MONOGRAPHS OF THE
SOCIETY FOR RESEARCH IN
CHILD DEVELOPMENT

*Serial No. 260, Vol. 65, No. 1, 2000*

# MAKING THE MOST OF SUMMER SCHOOL: A META-ANALYTIC AND NARRATIVE REVIEW

*Harris Cooper*
*Kelly Charlton*
*Jeff C. Valentine*
*Laura Muhlenbruck*

**WITH COMMENTARY BY**
*Geoffrey D. Borman*

MONOGRAPHS OF THE SOCIETY FOR RESEARCH IN CHILD DEVELOPMENT
*Serial No. 260, Vol. 65, No. 1, 2000*

# CONTENTS

# ABSTRACT

COOPER, HARRIS; CHARLTON, KELLY; VALENTINE, JEFF C.; and MUHLENBRUCK, LAURA. Making the Most of Summer School: A Meta-Analytic and Narrative Review. *Monographs of the Society for Research in Child Development*, 2000, **65**(1, Serial No. 260).

Summer schools serve multiple purposes for students, families, educators, and communities. The current need for summer programs is driven by changes in American families and by calls for an educational system that is competitive globally and embodies higher academic standards. A research synthesis is reported that used both meta-analytic and narrative procedures to integrate the results of 93 evaluations of summer school. Results revealed that summer programs focusing on remedial or accelerated learning or other goals have a positive impact on the knowledge and skills of participants. Although all students benefit from summer school, students from middle-class homes show larger positive effects than students from disadvantaged homes. Remedial programs have larger effects when the program is relatively small and when instruction is individualized. Remedial programs may have more positive effects on math than on reading. Requiring parent involvement also appears related to more effective programs. Students at all grade levels benefit from remedial summer school, but students in the earliest grades and in secondary school may benefit most. These and other findings are examined for their implications for future research, public policy, and the implementation of summer programs.

Based on these results, our recommendations to policy makers are that summer programs (a) contain substantial components aimed at teaching math and reading and (b) include rigorous evaluations, but also (c) permit local control of curricula and delivery systems. Funds should be set aside to foster participation in summer programs, especially among disadvantaged youth. Program implementers should (a) begin summer program planning earlier in the year, (b) strive for continuity of staffing and programs across years, (c) use summer school in conjunction with summer staff development opportunities, and (d) begin integrating summer school experiences with those that occur during the regular school year.

# I. INTRODUCTION

Summertime, and the livin' is easy,
Fish are jumpin', and the cotton is high.

"Summertime" by George Gershwin (1935)

For most American children prior to 1935, Gershwin's lyrics did not capture the experience of summer as they knew it. In the 19th century, if children lived in agricultural areas, summertime meant helping tend crops or livestock around the farm. If children lived in urban areas, it was not unusual to attend school for at least 2 of summer's 3 months (Richmond, 1977). By the turn of the century, implementation of standardized school curricula and family mobility resulted in the current 9-month calendar, and summer became a time without school for children (Association of California School Administrators, 1988). Still, most children were immigrants from abroad who made their homes in large urban areas or they were part of the great migration of Americans from the farm to the city. For them, fish jumpin' and high cotton were things heard about in song, not experienced in everyday life.

If Gershwin's bucolic picture missed the mark, Hans Carste and Charles Tobias' ode to "those lazy, hazy, crazy days of summer" (recorded by Nat King Cole in 1962) was not much more accurate. As Dougherty (1981) pointed out, in the early 20th century, many children held jobs during the summer and those who were idle were a cause of concern for city dwellers. The passage of the first child labor law in 1916 meant that school-aged children had little, if anything, to do during their vacation from school. Community leaders demanded that organized recreational activities be made available for students when school was out. Education officials responded by creating the first summer programs. The programs initially were heavily recreational, but as time passed, educators came to see summer as an opportunity to increase students' interest in lifelong learning.

1

## OBJECTIVES OF THE RESEARCH SYNTHESIS

*Our primary goal in conducting this research synthesis was to gather, summarize, critically analyze, and integrate the research literature concerning the effects of summer school on children and adolescents.* A good research synthesis should include both analytic and synthetic components. Analytically, it should point out and clarify, when possible, inconsistencies in the literature. One of our objectives, then, was to critically examine the research on summer school with an eye toward understanding why inconsistent results appear and how the methods chosen to study summer school might facilitate or restrict our ability to draw trustworthy inferences about program effects.

Synthetically, a good research synthesis should bring together what is known about a topic in the most parsimonious manner possible. In our case, this involved seeking an answer to the broadest question about summer school and also discovering the qualifications and caveats that restrict or specify that answer. Thus, we attempted to answer the question "What are the overall effects of summer school on children and adolescents?" We also sought qualifications to our response by answering the question "What characteristics of students, programs, and outcomes are associated with more or less effective summer programs?" The final characteristic of a good synthesis is that it should instigate a progressive paradigm shift (Strike & Posner, 1983). When our synthesis of summer school was complete, we hoped it would more broadly integrate the summer school literature with other related research literatures, invigorate future research by pointing to exciting and informative issues yet to be resolved, and reveal clear prescriptions for action on the part of policy makers and practitioners. Thus, we sought to answer the question "What does research say needs to be done to make the most of summer school?"

To accomplish our objectives, we begin by describing the history of summer school and the multiple purposes it has come to serve for students and communities. Then, we outline the forces creating the current and future need for school-based summer programs. Third, the results of past syntheses of research are described. Fourth, we examine the difficulties involved in studying whether summer schools accomplish their goals. As the core of this *Monograph*, we analyze and synthesize the empirical research that evaluates summer school. Finally, we interpret the research summary, suggest directions for future research, and propose guidelines for both policy makers and practitioners about how to implement effective summer school programs.

*The secondary goal of our synthesis was to introduce or demonstrate a set of valuable research synthesis techniques that are either underutilized or not well understood.* First and foremost, we attempted to fully integrate the use of both quantitative and narrative techniques so that our conclusions about summer school could take advantage of the strengths of both approaches to research synthesis (cf. Slavin, 1986). In the pages that follow, we provide narrative descriptions of most summer school evaluations. The descriptions, however, are embedded within the results of a meta-analysis. We refer to each study when the quantitative synthesis suggests the study made its strongest or most unique contribution to the literature. Also, we describe the results of each study not in terms of the statistical significance of its results, but with regard to the magnitude of the effect of summer school it revealed. Thus, the narrative descriptions place the results of studies in the currency of meta-analysis.

Also, we demonstrate four less-well-known and less-used quantitative approaches to synthesizing a research literature. First, in the course of conducting a meta-analysis, synthesists frequently find empirical studies that tell the direction of a treatment's effect but do not contain enough information for the calculation of effect sizes. Typically, these studies are discarded or (questionable) assumptions are made to generate effect sizes from them (e.g., the effect size is set to zero). We use these studies to demonstrate a procedure for obtaining a rough estimate of the average effect size underlying the set of direction-only studies, even though no single study in the set permits the calculation of its own effect size result.

Second, we apply both fixed-effect and random-effect models of error variance to the summer school data set. We leave the more technical description of these models to later in this report. At this point, suffice it to say that interest in random-effect models for the study of interventions such as summer school is increasing, because meta-analysts are becoming more discriminating in their choices of statistical models and procedures for conducting random-effect analyses are becoming more accessible. By juxtaposing the results of the two approaches, we hope to make them more accessible and to bring the differences between them into clearer focus.

Third, it is typically the case that the variables of substantive interest in a research synthesis (e.g., whether summer programs are more effective for regular students or students with special needs) are confounded in study designs with methodological variations (e.g., how carefully summer school participants and control students were equated). In this synthesis we demonstrate a simple but rarely used technique for adjusting effect sizes to remove the covariance between methodological and substantive characteristics within the meta-analytic data set.

Finally, we show how to carry out a meta-analytic procedure that takes advantage of the fact that some studies contain within them variations of substantive interest to the synthesist. As our example, we found a set of studies that measured the effect of summer school on both reading and math. These studies provide for stronger causal inferences because most, if not all, other methodological, student, program, and outcome variations are held constant when effects on reading and math are compared. When multiple studies with within-study comparisons are available, meta-analysts can take advantage of them to draw stronger inferences.

## HISTORY AND GOALS OF SUMMER SCHOOL

Today, the purposes of summer programs stretch far beyond making organized recreational activities available to students out of school. The *prevention of delinquent behavior*, however, certainly remains among summer school's latent functions. Furthermore, it is not unusual to find summer programs with a component that attempts to *build positive attitudes toward self and learning* to lessen the chances of antisocial behaviors in the future.

Although keeping kids off the street provided the initial impetus for summer school, by the 1950s educators realized that summer schools could furnish opportunities to *remediate or prevent learning deficits* (Austin, Rogers, & Walbesser, 1972). Because the wealthy were able to hire tutors for their children, the educational summer programs made available through schools largely served students from disadvantaged backgrounds.

Summer programs to remediate learning deficits can be grouped into four categories. First, some summer programs are meant to help students meet minimum competency requirements for graduation or grade promotion. Most states set minimum competency standards for obtaining a high school diploma. When a student does not meet the standards, summer schools provide an excellent opportunity for the intensive instruction needed to raise the specific competencies above the required minimum.

Second, students who fail a particular course during the regular academic year use summer school as an opportunity to retake the course. Repetition of failed courses occurs primarily at the secondary level. The related remedial activity in elementary grades occurs when students are requested or required to take summer instruction in order to avoid being retained at the same grade level during the next school year.

Third, the movement to insure that students with disabilities receive a free and appropriate education (FAPE) resulted in the passage in 1975 of the Individuals with Disabilities Education Act (IDEA; Public Law 94-142). Prior to 1975, approximately 1 million children with disabilities were excluded entirely from public education, and more than half of all children with disabilities did not receive appropriate educational services (*Federal Register*, Vol. 62, No. 204, 1997). In 1979, the United States District Court ruled that the Pennsylvania Department of Education had to provide a program beyond the regular school year for children with disabilities. The

4

ruling was based on the premise that the long summer break would lead to regression of skills in students covered by the IDEA. The 1997 proposed rules for the reauthorized IDEA (Public Law 105-17) stated that ". . . each public agency shall ensure that extended year services are available to each child with a disability to the extent necessary to ensure that FAPE is available to the child" (*Federal Register*, Vol. 62, No. 204, Section, 300.309, 1997). The rules also stated that the determination of the extent of these services must be made on an individual basis and be provided at no expense to the child's parents. Thus, the law mandates that school-based and government-financed summer programs be provided for certain students with disabilities.

Additionally, the Elementary and Secondary Education Act of 1965 (ESEA; Public Law 89-10) included funds for programs to meet educational needs identified as national priorities. Title I of the law recognized the special needs of students residing in areas with high concentrations of poverty. Title I programs were meant to break the self-perpetuating cycle of poverty through the provision of supplemental educational services. The 1994 reauthorization of ESEA, entitled the Improving America's Schools Act (Public Law 103-382), continued the Title I emphasis on closing the achievement gap between rich and poor. To accomplish this goal, Section 1001(c)(4) stated that resources are best spent when "used to ensure that children have full access to effective high-quality regular school programs and *receive supplemental help through extended time activities*" (emphasis added). This federal mandate, along with others created by state and local education agencies, has led to the use of Title I funds to establish summer programs for disadvantaged youth. These summer programs focus on both the prevention and/or remediation of learning deficiencies. In addition, separate federal and state legislation focuses on the unique needs of children of migrant workers. Although these programs focus on both reading and math (Heyns, 1986), they often include unique components meant to teach English language skills to students who speak Spanish at home.

Dougherty (1981) pointed to the publication of James B. Conant's (1959) book *The American High School* as another turning point in thinking about summer school. Conant recommended that boards of education provide summer opportunities not only for students who were struggling in school but also for those who needed more *flexible course schedules* or who sought *enriched educational experiences*. This would be accomplished by providing summer opportunities to take courses given during the regular school year that could not be fit into a student's regular program of study. Conant suggested students who were heavily involved in extracurricular activities or who held work-study positions could use summer school as a way to lighten their academic burden without delaying their graduation. Students who wished to graduate early could use summer school to speed up their

5

accumulation of credits. School administrators in the 1960s, faced with the space crunch created by the baby boom, saw the use of summer school to speed up graduation as a way to make more room for the growing number of students.

The summer vacation also has been embraced as an ideal time to *provide specialized programs for students with academic gifts and other talents.* Such programs often involve offering advanced instruction that goes beyond the typical school course of study. At the high school level, the content of these courses might be based on college-level curricula. Other programs take students with special talents to college during summer and provide in-residence programs.

Summer school also has been recognized as providing opportunities for teachers. Summer schools *offer teachers an opportunity to make additional money and to develop professional competencies.* Although many teachers look toward summer as a time for relaxation, recreation, and rejuvenation, others use the opportunity to teach in summer as a way to supplement their income and to develop additional expertise.

*Summer learning loss.* A final rationale for summer school that has recently gained attention concerns the phenomenon of summer learning loss. A research synthesis conducted by Cooper, Nye, Charlton, Lindsay, and Greathouse (1996) helped kindle interest in this issue. These researchers integrated 39 studies examining the effects of summer vacation on achievement test scores. Their meta-analysis indicated that summer learning loss equaled at least 1 month of instruction. On average, children's test scores were at least 1 month lower when they return to school in fall than scores were when students left in spring.

This meta-analysis also found dramatic differences in the effect of summer vacation on different skill areas. Summer loss was more pronounced for math than for reading and math facts, and spelling showed much larger losses than other subject areas. To explain this finding, the authors suggested that both math facts and spelling skills involve the acquisition of factual and procedural knowledge, whereas other skill areas, especially math concepts and problem solving and reading comprehension, are more conceptually based. Without practice, cognitive psychology suggests, facts and procedural skills are most susceptible to forgetting. The authors speculated that children's home environments provide more opportunities to practice reading skills than to practice mathematics.

In addition to the influence of subject area, the researchers had examined numerous differences among students as moderators of summer vacations' effect. Overall, the meta-analysis revealed little evidence to suggest that student intelligence had an impact on the effect of summer break. Also, neither the student's gender nor ethnicity appeared to have a consistent influence on the summer learning loss, although educators express special concern, likely legitimate, about the impact of summer vacation on the language skills of students who do not speak English at home.

Finally, family economics was examined as an influence on summer learning loss. The meta-analysis revealed that all students, regardless of economic group, lost roughly equal amounts of math skills over summer. Substantial differences, however, were found for reading. On some measures, middle-class children showed gains in reading achievement over summer, but disadvantaged children showed losses. Reading comprehension scores of both income groups declined, but more so for disadvantaged students. Thus, income differences appear to be related to differences in opportunities to practice and learn reading skills over summer; more books and reading opportunities are available to middle-class children.

Cooper et al. (1996) proposed two approaches to the alleviation of summer learning loss. First, the existence of summer learning loss could be used to argue for adopting changes in the school calendar (see Worsnop, 1996). Second, the summer loss suggested the continuation of summer remedial and enrichment programs. For all students, the authors suggested, a primary focus on mathematics instruction in summer would seem to be needed the most. If programs had the explicit purpose of lessening inequities across income groups, then a focus on summer reading instruction for disadvantaged students would be most beneficial.

Cooper and colleagues were quick to point out that the existence of summer learning loss could not ipso facto be taken to mean their proposed solutions would be effective remedial interventions. The review of summer loss did "not estimate how much, if any, of the summer loss could be recouped by adding days to the school year" (p. 264). The impact of alternative school calendars and summer educational programs had to be evaluated on their own merits. Thus, the need for quality research and research syntheses was established.


## CURRENT AND FUTURE NEEDS FOR SUMMER SCHOOL

Throughout this century, the purposes of summer schools have expanded from the initial goal of preventing delinquency to include remediation and prevention of learning deficiencies, flexible scheduling, academic enrichment and acceleration, summer employment for teachers, and the mitigation of summer learning loss. There is good reason to believe that expansion of both the goals and availability of summer school will continue throughout the next several decades. We base this prediction on three national trends.

*Changes in the American family.* First, the nature of the American family has undergone dramatic changes. Reynolds Farley (1996), using the last four U.S. Censuses as his starting point, summed up these changes:

> . . . the living arrangements of children and their parents in the 1990s are quite different from those of children and parents three decades ago. Then, the image of the typical American family included an employed father, a home-maker wife, and two children. There is no such popular image of the typical family today. Many families continue to resemble that 1950s icon, but they are in the minority, and their number is decreasing steadily. Much more common is the family in which both parents work or, increasingly, the family headed by a single parent. Most children born in the 1980s and 1990s will live in a single-parent family for some time before they graduate high school. (p. 108)

Farley further pointed out that in 1990 almost half of mother-only families existed below the poverty line.

The changes in American families suggest that the years ahead will bring increasing demands for government-sponsored, school-based services for children when regular classes are not in session. Advocates for children living in families that lack the resources to provide quality educational and recreational activities will lead the call for quality programming when school is out. Families that do have adequate resources, however, are likely to request these services as well. The growing number of middle-class families in which no adult is home during the day suggests that these families may increase their reliance on organized summer programs offered by schools, be they free or tuition-based.

It seems reasonable to assume that along with the increased demand for more summer school opportunities will come new purposes added to the existing menu. Specifically, we might expect summer programs to begin to focus on teaching a wide array of life skills formerly thought to be the province of families. These would include teaching children positive character traits, physical or athletic skills, and how to maintain their health.

*Maintenance of a globally competitive education system.* Although additional purposes for summer school will emerge, the primary focus is likely to remain academic. In the past 2 decades, many policy makers have become concerned about the global competitiveness of the American economy and the education system that drives it (National Commission on Excellence in Education, 1983). These concerns have focused considerable attention on the relatively short American school year. Writing in the *Atlantic Monthly*, Michael J. Barrett (1990), a former Massachusetts state senator and unsuccessful gubernatorial candidate in 1994, summarized this concern:

The United States faces a time-in-school deficit every bit as serious as the trade deficit and the balance-of-payments problem: each year, American children receive hundreds of hours less schooling than many of their European and Asian mates, and the resulting harm promises to be cumulative and lasting. (p. 86)

Stevenson and Lee (1990), in a *Monograph* entitled "Contexts of Achievement" (that also appeared in this series), documented Barrett's concern. These researchers compared the number of days students spent in school in three countries. They found that the length of the school year was 230 days in Taipei, Taiwan, 243 days in Sendai, China, and 174 days in Minneapolis, Minnesota. Students in Taipei and Sendai attended school for a half-day on Saturday. When Stevenson and Lee totaled the number of hours spent in school each year in the three countries, they found a roughly equal number of hours for 1st graders (because the Minneapolis school day was longer), but considerably fewer hours for Minneapolis 5th graders. Whereas Minneapolis 5th graders spent about 1,044 hours in school each year, Sendai students spent about 1,466 hours and Taipei students spent about 1,655.

Also related to the need for summer school in the United States was Stevenson and Lee's finding that "American mothers may be dedicated to their child's development during his or her preschool years but . . . they abdicate some of these responsibilities to the teacher once the child enters school. This trend is opposite from that which occurs in Chinese and Japanese families. . . ." (p. 100). Finally, students in the two Asian cities were found to spend more out-of-school time doing homework and reading than did Minneapolis students.

We should point out that Stevenson and Lee did not conclude that insufficient time and emphasis devoted to academic activities was the sole factor related to the Minneapolis students' relatively poor performance compared to their Asian counterparts, although it was first on their list (p. 103). They also indict inefficient use of time, low standards, and a lack of parent involvement, among others.

*Establishment of high standards and minimum competency requirements.* In addition to issues of global competitiveness, an emphasis has emerged nationally on higher academic standards and minimum competency requirements. The new standards and requirements have provided impetus for increased use of summer schools (Chmelynski, 1998). For example, Chicago Public Schools has a policy that establishes districtwide standards of promotion for students completing 3rd, 6th, and 8th grades. If students do not meet minimum grade-equivalent reading and math scores, report card grades, and attendance criteria, they are either retained or must attend the

Summer Bridge Program. The policy was meant to "end the practice of social promotion and will better prepare students for success at the next organizational level" (Chicago Public Schools, 1997, p. 3). In 1998, 60,000 Chicago students were summoned to summer school. In all, about 175,000 of Chicago's 430,000 students took part in all its summer programs, including special, bilingual, and gifted education and recreational programs (White, 1998). Similar revitalized programs of both mandatory and recommended summer remedial education are in operation in Washington, D.C., Denver, and Milwaukee public schools.

In sum then, impetus for more schooling opportunities in summer exists today and should increase for the foreseeable future. The push for more summer learning opportunities for children and adolescents will gather momentum from changes in the American family that create new demands on schools and from a political focus on increasing the number of days children spend in formal education as a means for meeting higher academic standards and improving America's global economic position.

## PAST REVIEWS OF SUMMER SCHOOL RESEARCH

Previous reviews of research on summer school are scarce. In the early 1970s, Austin, Rogers, and Walbesser (1972) reviewed research on summer programs for students eligible for Title I services. They concluded that summer compensatory education programs "in elementary mathematics, reading, and language-communication have generally shown modest achievement gains" (p. 179). They noted, however, that because none of the evaluations they reviewed employed random assignment, maturation remained a threat to validity. Also, there was no evidence on whether summer school effects persisted over time. With regard to attitudinal measures, the reviewers concluded that summer school had positive effects on students' desire to attend school and learn but no evidence was available on whether these attitudes translated into changed behavior. Finally, Austin and colleagues noted that few summer programs had goals that were stated clearly to help guide evaluations, and many projects claimed funding arrived too late to allow for proper evaluation.

Heyns (1986) provided a review of summer compensatory education programs. She pointed out that there was a dearth of data on summer school programs and their effectiveness and no taxonomy existed for cataloging summer programs in a fashion that would lead to meaningful data on these issues. Based on data collected in the mid-1970s, Heyns reported that about half of school districts in the United States made summer school available and about half of these programs were entirely compensatory in nature. About one third of programs had both compensatory and enrichment components and one sixth were exclusively enrichment. Heyns went on to describe the historical background of summer programs for preschool children, Title I programs for both regular and migrant youth, and programs for students with special learning needs. Heyns stated that "with regard to summer programs [for Title I regular students], it is clear we know next to nothing about the distribution or effects of compensatory education" (p. III–11). Although better data were available at the state level on summer programs for children of migrant workers, Heyns judged these data to be largely incommensurate across states. Finally, Heyns found the literature on summer programs for children with special needs to be largely descriptive, with no experimental studies yet available. The last half of Heyns' chapter was devoted to an analysis of summer learning gains and losses. She stated that "we stand to learn more about intellectual development and cognitive growth by studying summer learning than by any other means" (p. III–15).

Ascher (1988) provided a brief review of research on summer schools, extended school years, and alternative school calendars for disadvantaged students. The review was prepared for the ERIC Clearinghouse on Urban Education. She concluded that attending summer school led to only modest improvements in elementary school students' achievement and at disproportionately high cost, although no cost-benefit analysis was presented in the paper. Ascher also stated that "we know almost nothing about summer programs for disadvantaged middle and high school students" (p. 1). She noted, however, that the poor results "can be at least partly attributed to the current programs themselves" (p. 1). Problems with programs include short duration, loose organization, little time for advanced planning, low academic expectations, discontinuity between summer and regular school year curriculum, time wasted as new teachers get to know students, teacher fatigue, and poor attendance.

These three reviews are now seriously dated. More than a decade has passed since the last appeared. Furthermore, none of the reviews claimed to be based on thorough searches of research sources. Finally, none used meta-analysis techniques to integrate the results of the included studies. All three reviews correctly suggested that even a thorough search followed by powerful synthesis tools would face numerous challenges because of the diversity among summer school programs and weaknesses in research. We turn our attention now to some of these challenges.

## ISSUES IN SUMMER SCHOOL RESEARCH

Before examining the research in detail, it is important to set out some of the major issues researchers and research interpreters confront when attempting to evaluate the effectiveness of summer school. We can identify four interrelated issues that deserve special consideration.

*Criteria for success.* The variety of goals for summer school suggests that we will encounter equal variety when cataloging the criteria researchers have used to determine whether or not a particular program has been successful. Interestingly, we found no instance in which a measure of *delinquency* during the summer program was used as an indicator of program success. These measures might include archival data, such as the arrest records of summer school participants. Occasionally, measures of the effects of summer school on factors related to delinquency, such as past participants' *absenteeism, self-esteem,* and *attitudes toward school,* have appeared in the literature.

With regard to *academic indices* of success, researchers have used criteria as simple as the percentage of students mastering learning objectives during the summer session or the percentage of students successfully completing a previously failed course. These percentages were compared to a specified percentage that was set by program overseers or evaluators. If the percentage was surpassed, the program was deemed a success.

The percentage-mastery criteria have the advantage of being both practical and easy to interpret. Their problem is that the specified percentage for declaring success can be set low, and at different benchmarks for different programs or for the same program in different years. This permits a host of subjective considerations to enter the evaluation process, sometimes predetermining the outcome. We found no evaluation of a summer program that used a percentage-mastery criterion that deemed the summer program a failure.

Also, without a specific comparison group, it is not clear how students who attend summer programs ultimately differed from nonparticipants with similar educational needs. For example, it may be the case that the gains in mastery of reading objectives attained by a 1st grader in summer school are mirrored by similar children not attending summer school, simply because of emerging developmental skills or opportunities inherent in children's environments. Or high school students who retake a course in summer may be no more likely to persist to graduation than other failing students who retake the course during the regular school year. Our intuition tells us such instances are rare; the percentage-mastery criteria leave these critical numbers unmeasured. Thus, based on the unscientific nature of their comparison group, we chose to exclude studies that used the percentage-mastery criterion to assess the success of a summer program.

By far, the most frequent measures of summer school success involve a comparison of student achievement test scores either (a) from the same students before and after attending summer school or (b) from students who did or did not attend summer school. The outcome measures use raw scores or norm-reference indices, such as grade-level equivalents. If the summer school students' pretest score is lower than the posttest score, or if students attending summer school score higher than students not attending summer school, then the program is deemed a success.

*The choice of comparison groups.* When success is defined in relative terms, the critical question becomes "relative to what?" Following the logic of Campbell and Stanley (1966; also see Cook & Campbell, 1979) the weakest comparison from which to draw inferences about program success is the one-group (in this case, summer school attendees) pretest-posttest comparison.

As with the percentage-mastery criteria, the *one-group pretest-posttest comparison* leaves unanswered the question of how much change occurred during the same time period among similar students not involved in summer school. In this case, the existence of summer learning loss raises the distinct possibility that a pretest-posttest comparison for students who do not attend summer school would show a decline in achievement scores. Therefore, a one-group pretest-posttest comparison that indicated a summer program was associated with "no gain but no loss" might be improperly deemed a failure. It also may be misleading, however, to decide that "no change" from pretest to posttest necessarily means a program was a success. The existence or amount of summer learning loss we might expect would be very difficult to predict, because the loss will vary by subject matter and the students' economic status, in addition to the vagaries of statistical sampling and measurement reliability. Furthermore, one-group pretest-posttest designs are open to history, testing, and maturation influences, as well as possible regression to the mean, if students were chosen for summer school based on extremely low pretest scores.

Finally, the one-group pretest-posttest design can be misleading if the measure of achievement involves grade-level equivalent scores or some other form of normed-referenced index. Cooper et al. (1996) examined this issue in detail. Briefly, depending on the time interval between pretest and posttest, it is not impossible that grade-level equivalent scores could indicate a gain in achievement (say, from grade level 5.8 to 6.0) without any actual gain in skill or knowledge. This can happen because (a) the norming process adjusted the scale to remove summer learning loss or (b) there existed variable rates of learning at different times of the school year. Thus, a summer program might appear effective when, in fact, no learning gain had occurred.

For these reasons, the one-group pretest-posttest design provides an equivocal comparison for drawing inferences about program success. Its strength lies in our knowledge of the comparability of the pretest and posttest groups, because they are the same students. Its weakness lies in the confound of the treatment with the passage of time between testings. We shall see that many evaluations of summer school employ this design, probably because of the ease of its implementation

Other designs used to assess the effects of summer school compare students who did and did not attend a program. In the best case, the *comparison groups are determined by randomly picking program participants* from a longer list of students who wished to go to summer school. Then, the researcher compares postprogram scores for the picked and not-picked students.

A design of near-equal inferential power involves *identifying students who are eligible for summer school and then inviting a random subset.* Care must be taken in this design to track the number of invitees who refuse the offer. As the number of refusals increases, so do differences between students who chose to attend and students not invited.

The use of random assignment in evaluations of summer school is rare, probably because denying access to a summer program on a random basis is politically untenable for schools and districts, unless more students want access than can be accommodated by the program. Therefore, less preferable methods are often used to constitute a group to compare to students who attend summer school. These methods involve using *matching or post hoc statistical procedures to enhance the comparability of program participants and nonparticipants.* Such procedures vary in rigor from study to study. For example, some investigators compare the postprogram test scores of students who attend summer school with districtwide average test scores of students in the same grade. Others compare program participants with nonparticipants equated according to district, grade, achievement level, sex, ethnic group, and/or socioeconomic status.

The validity of these nonequivalent control group designs is a direct function of the care taken in the matching procedures. Obviously, the more numerous and relevant the equating variables, the more certain we can be that any postprogram differences are actually due to summer school and not to preexisting differences between students. Our certainty using this design, however, never reaches the level achieved by the use of random-assignment procedures (see Cook & Campbell, 1979, for a thorough discussion). The simple fact that summer school participants are motivated to attend the program often sets them apart from their peers in an important, perhaps critical, way. Measuring motivation-to-learn, however, often is difficult and costly. We found no instance in which researchers were able to equate nonrandomly assigned groups of participants and nonparticipants according to their level of motivation to do well in school.

*Program persistence and attendance.* Related to the issue of motivation is that of persistence among students who are in a summer program. Summer school is often optional and there are many enticements to drop out or skip class. Therefore, program implementers often face high attrition and absence rates. Evaluators are confronted with the dilemma of whether to include in their data analyses students enrolled in the program who had poor attendance records. We found that some researchers include all students but others set an arbitrary attendance cut-off. The cut-off differed from study to study.

*The congruence between program goals and outcome measures.* Finally, an important consideration in summer school research concerns the correspondence between what the program hoped to accomplish and what was measured at the program's conclusion. As Austin and colleagues (1972) pointed out, when planning an evaluation it is important to make explicit the program's goals and to identify and measure those student outcomes most directly tied to these goals. Often, researchers measure outcomes with tenuous conceptual links to the program goals. In many evaluations a post-program test battery is given, because it is conveniently administered as a unit or it is part of a district's regular testing program. Evaluators then compared students on a variety of measures. When this occurs, an interpretation of the evidence requires distinguishing those outcomes expected to respond to the program's content from those for which an effect was less likely.

*A note on the value of a research synthesis.* Given the diversity of summer program goals and components, and given the litany of methodological concerns we have outlined, we might now ask whether anything at all is to be gained from an attempt to synthesize the summer school research. It is a fair question.

We think there are two excellent reasons to press ahead. First, research synthesists can examine what the implications of methodological variations are for the results of studies if they pay careful attention to the details of research methodology in their search for moderators of treatment effects. When results reveal themselves to be robust across different methods that engender different threats to the validity of inferences, then more confident conclusions can be drawn, even in the absence of tightly controlled experiments. When a subset of tightly controlled experiments is available (as it is here), these results can be compared to those of less rigorous designs. If studies differ in both rigor and results, then the synthesists' conclusions can be weighted to favor the more rigorous designs. A careful and critical analysis of how design features relate to study results is the unique province of research synthesis and one that can lead to inferences far more trustworthy than those arising from any single study.

Our second rationale for pressing forward is more pragmatic. Each day, policies and practices for summer schools are under construction. All too often, these decisions are made based on little knowledge gleaned from research. Although federal, state, and local officials, curriculum specialists, and teachers make decisions informed by their personal experiences, they often benefit little from the cumulative knowledge of others. We most certainly agree that "bad evidence is worse than no evidence." Researchers know, however, that if there are some kernels of insight they can add to the decision-making process, they ought to do so. Well-conducted research syntheses are one way to uncover these insights. The process of decision making about whether and how to implement summer programs will go on with or without the participation of the research community.

## PREDICTIONS ABOUT THE EFFECTS OF SUMMER SCHOOL

The variety of goals for summer school and the complexities of researching its effectiveness mean that predictions about evaluation results will require attention to a host of moderating influences. In addition to goals, influences on evaluations will include the metric of the outcome measurements, the correspondence between goals and outcomes, the level of student participation, the achievement level and economic circumstances of participants, and, perhaps most critically, the nature of the comparison group. Moreover, these influences not only can have simple effects, but also can interact with one another. We will illustrate this complexity by considering only a few variations on predictions for one subject (reading), and two groups of students (elementary-school children from disadvantaged and middle-class backgrounds).

We can predict that summer reading programs will have positive effects on disadvantaged children when program success is defined as the mastery of a small number of reading skills. If outcomes are measured by comparing student postprogram scores to preprogram scores on standardized tests, we might expect that, for students from low-income backgrounds, the absence of a summer loss also indicates a program has been successful. A similar "no change" result for middle-class children, however, might suggest the reading program was not successful. The summer loss literature suggests positive change on selected reading abilities should occur for middle-class students even in the absence of summer school. Predictions become more difficult if evaluators employ norm-referenced test scores. A gain of 1 month on grade-level equivalent scales essentially suggests that students have not changed their place in the distribution relative to the norming group. A change of more or less than 1 month is inherently ambiguous, because it must be interpreted against (a) whether the test adjusted upward raw scores that revealed summer loss and (b) the length of the norming interval (typically, mid-fall and mid-spring) relative to the length of the summer testing interval.

Certainly, we can conclude a summer program is effective if randomly assigned participants outperform their nonparticipating counterparts. We should expect an even larger effect of participation when summer school students are compared to nonparticipating students who have been matched on gender, economic, and/or achievement factors, but not on motivation. There is less reason, however, to expect conclusions will be favorable to a summer program when comparing low-income students' postprogram scores to districtwide average scores obtained at the same time. Again, summer loss research suggests that districtwide averages may include many nonparticipating students for whom reading improvements continue over summer, because they have greater economic support at home than program participants. This will be true even when achievement scores for both groups have been adjusted for initial achievement differences. We would expect the opposite relation to exist when middle-class students who attend summer school are compared to districtwide averages. The middle-class students then have both the program and their home environment working to their relative advantage.

We could continue to posit predictions. Most of the multitude of permutations of interacting influences, however, have no or few empirical testings described in the research literature. Rather than belabor the point, we now turn to a description and integration of research assessing the effectiveness of summer school programs.

# II. LITERATURE SEARCH AND DATABASE CONSTRUCTION

## CRITERIA FOR INCLUDING STUDIES

Studies included in the synthesis had to meet several criteria. First, the program had to take place during the summer vacation, when regular school was not in session. Second, we included studies involving students in kindergarten through 12th grade. Preschool and postsecondary summer school programs were not included. Third, programs for both regular students and special needs students, that is, programs for students with learning, physical, emotional, or behavioral disabilities, were included in the database.

Fourth, the study had to focus on the evaluation of a program organized by a school, school district, college, or university. Programs exclusively run by private groups, for example, for-profit tutoring or college entrance exam courses, were excluded from the database, but public/private partnerships, for example, programs that included half-day instruction along with half-day employment or programs jointly funded by public and philanthropic organizations, were included.

Fifth, the program had to have goals associated with preventing delinquent behavior or improving academic performance or school attendance. Goals could be measured directly, for example, using achievement tests, or indirectly, for example, using measures of self-esteem. Programs with other types of goals, for example, reduction of prejudice or career planning, were not included in the database.

Sixth, the study had to compare the effects of attending versus not attending a summer program, either by preprogram versus postprogram comparison or a comparison between two groups. For example, a study was excluded if it only looked at individual differences between students who did or did not attend summer school; that is, it examined the question "Who decides to go to summer school?" without examining the effect of summer school on attendees. It was included if it compared the effects of summer school on students with different characteristics, say males versus females.

Seventh, the study had to test empirically the effects of the summer program. We found some reports that included only descriptions of programs or that said empirical evaluations were carried out but did not report the direction and/or statistical outcomes of the evaluation. These reports were not included in the database. Also, for reasons outlined in our introduction, we excluded studies that compared students who attended summer school against a preestablished mastery criterion for measuring success.

Finally, the study had to include an outcome measure taken on the students who attended the program. We excluded studies that focused exclusively on parents or teachers. The descriptions of included studies provided below, however, do make reference to measures taken on parents and teachers when these were included in studies that focused on student outcomes. No study was dropped from the meta-analysis based on the exclusive use teachers or parents, because there was always at least one other reason present for the study's exclusion.

## LITERATURE SEARCH PROCEDURES

We used two strategies to locate evaluations of summer school programs. First, we ran computer searches of the ERIC and PsychINFO reference databases. The ERIC database was searched for the period January 1966 to August 1998. The PsychINFO database was searched for the period January 1967 to August 1998. We used the search terms "summer school," "summer program," and "compensatory education" along with "summer" when searching both reference databases. After identifying 5,111 documents through ERIC and 236 through PsychINFO, we limited our search further to only those documents that referred to programs involving school-aged children. The search of ERIC identified 2,065 document records that contained at least one of the search terms. The PsychINFO search identified 131 documents.

Two authors then reviewed the abstract of each record. We retrieved the complete document if either author believed the document might contain an empirical evaluation of the effects of summer school. This led us to review 258 full documents. Also, we examined the reference sections of reports that included empirical comparisons to determine if reference was made to other potentially relevant reports. We examined 75 reports found in other reference lists but not in the reference databases. A very few reports we would have liked to examine could not be obtained through our library or interlibrary loan.

Solicitation letters to active researchers in the field were not sent because we found no evidence that particular researchers pursued summer school evaluations on a continuing basis. We did, however, receive several leads and unsolicited documents from researchers who were aware of our project.

Certainly, all evaluations of summer school programs will not be located by searching reference databases and reference lists and bias against the null hypothesis is always a concern when research synthesists gather literature. It is also the case, however, that bias against the null hypothesis is of most concern when authors submit and editors review manuscripts for publication in scientific journals. The summer school literature contains few published studies; it is composed predominantly of documents prepared for use by school districts and government agencies and these documents often do not even contain statistical inference tests. Therefore, we suspect that bias against the null hypothesis is minimal in this literature.

### Coding Frame

In many cases, characteristics of each study could be retrieved directly from the research reports with no inferences made by the coders. Information such as the sample size and the duration of the program was of this sort. In cases where some inference was necessary, we relied, first, on our own definitions of categories to code studies and, second, on definitions provided by the report writers, when no other information was available. For instance, with regard to a sample's economic background, if the sample was described as composed of children eligible to participate in a free lunch program or if data were given indicating that the average family in the sample earned income below the poverty line, we classified this sample as of "low socioeconomic status (SES)." If information about free lunch or family income was not given but the author said the students were drawn from a "poor" or "disadvantaged" neighborhood, the sample was also classified as low SES. Finally, we classified as low SES any program that was meant to serve children of migrant workers. Codes were left blank when reports did not contain enough information to make a confident judgment of a study's status on a characteristic.

Fifty-three different characteristics of each study were included in the database. The 53 characteristics could be classified as to whether they referred to aspects of (a) the research report, (b) the research design, (c) the sample of students, (d) the program's structure and content, or (e) the indicators of the outcome of the effectiveness of the summer program.

*Report characteristics.* Each database entry for a research report began with the name of the first author. Then, the type of report was coded as either a journal article (for published reports), dissertation, internal evaluation (typically a district level report), or external evaluation (when an evaluation of a summer program was contained in a document issued by a private research firm or government organization other than the program sponsor). The year that the report was issued also was coded.

*Research design.* The major research design feature we coded related to the nature of the comparison groups. Four types of comparisons were identified. "Pretest-posttest comparisons" occurred when the preprogram scores of a group of students served as the comparison for postprogram scores. "Experimental comparisons" occurred when groups attending and not attending summer school were constituted using random assignment procedures. "Nonequivalent-groups comparisons" occurred when postprogram scores of students attending summer school were compared to those of students not attending summer school but some process other than random assignment was used to constitute the two groups. Finally, we distinguished whether nonequivalent-groups comparisons involved control groups sampled at the same time as the summer school group or, if a cohort design was used, involved students of similar status to program participants in years past.

For all research designs, we determined whether students received a pretest and whether or not the pretest was identical or functionally equivalent to the primary outcome measure. If a pretest was given, we recorded whether it was used to equate program and control students either by a priori matching or as a covariate in statistical analyses. When equating procedures were used, we recorded the student characteristics used for matching (e.g., achievement, sex, ethnic group, economic background). We did not record school district and grade level as matching variables, because these were used to match students in all studies.

Next, we gave each independent sample a unique sample number. With regard to the size of the evaluation, we recorded the total number of students used in the data analysis. Then, we coded whether the report included an assessment of the fidelity of the program's implementation, whether student attendance was routinely monitored, and the program's overall drop-out rate, if given. We also used a simple "yes" or "no" code to tell us whether the analysis dropped students who did not meet an attendance criterion. Finally, we recorded the number of students in the summer program and the control group, if any.

*Student characteristics.* Students were distinguished by the lowest and highest grade included in the summer program, by the economic background of the families or community served (low, middle, or mixed economic sample, as defined above), by whether only males, only females, or both sexes were included in the sample, and by the achievement level of the participating students.

The achievement level of students was one of the most difficult variables to code, because of vague and overlapping terminology. We created six different codes to distinguish achievement levels. The sample was labeled "gifted" if students were selected into the program based on an exceptional academic talent, "average" if there were no restrictions on participation or if the sample mirrored the general school population, "at-risk" if the report writers used no more precise definition for children who were having difficulties in school or were identified as potentially experiencing difficulties, "below grade level or underachieving" if lower-than-expected test scores were used to identify potential summer school participants, "failed or retained" if students became eligible for summer school because they either failed a particular course or were to be retained in grade if they did not participate in the summer program, and "learning or otherwise disabled" if a specified learning disability or other physical or emotional challenge was required to participate in the program. When more than one label was applied to students in a report we used the label that seemed to most precisely define the students (e.g., "failed or retained" was more precise than "at-risk").

*Program characteristics.* The goals of the summer programs were categorized as "delinquency prevention," "promotion" after failure or retention, "remediation" of learning deficiencies among students who were below-average achievers, "prevention" of future academic problems, "improvement of attitudes" toward school, "academic enrichment" for all students, "development of underachievers" (that is, students with above average ability not realizing their potential), "acceleration" of academic progress for above average achievers, or a "combination" of the above. Obviously, these labels are far from mutually exclusive and most often we found ourselves at the mercy of the categorizations used in the evaluation reports.

We coded the year in which the program was offered and how many years the program had been in existence. The size of the community served by the summer program was categorized as either a large urban area, a small city (with populations between 100,000 and 500,000), a suburb, a rural community, or a mixture of community types. The number of students, schools, and classes in the program was recorded, if given. The number of students in the program could differ from the sample size if not all students in the program participated in the evaluation.

We categorized programs with regard to whether participation was stated by the evaluators to be either required of the student or participants were invited or encouraged to attend. The average size of a class was coded as well as whether students were in residence at the summer school or traveled back and forth from home each day. We coded whether teachers were certified and whether the program required some involvement on the part of parents including, for example, volunteering time, observing a class, or taking part in a parent-teacher conference. We recorded data concerning the length of the program each day, and the number of days the program was in operation. Also, we noted the date of the last day the summer school program met.

The program's curriculum was categorized according to whether it was structured for "group" or "individual" instruction. The subject focus of the program was coded as math, reading, writing, language, science, other, or various combinations of subjects.

*Outcome measures.* We recorded whether outcome measures were taken immediately after the summer program ended, early in the next fall (September or October), late in the next fall (November or December), during the next winter or spring, after 1 year, or after more than 1 year. Also, we coded whether the outcome measures were teacher-constructed or standardized tests, and if standardized tests were used whether they involved raw test scores or some scaled measurement, such as grade-level equivalent scores.

A wide variety of knowledge and skill areas were measured as outcomes of the summer program. Specific subject matter outcomes included overall mathematics tests scores, as well as subtests on math concepts, computation, and applications, and overall reading scores, as well as reading comprehension, word and paragraph meaning, vocabulary, spelling, and word sounds. General language and communication skills and science knowledge also served as outcome measures. More general academic measures included IQ scores, Scholastic Aptitude Test (SAT) scores, Cognitive Abilities Test (CAT) scores, and class standing. In the nonacademic domain, several studies measured student self-concept and others measured self-help skills or attitudes toward specific subject matters.

*Quantitative results.* With regard to the statistical results, for each comparison we retrieved the mean and standard deviation of the pretest and posttest for both the summer school and control groups, when available. Also, we recorded whether the specific comparison being coded involved a pretest and posttest from a summer school group or a posttest comparison between a summer school group and a control group. We had to make this code because the same sample could contribute both a pretest-posttest and a treatment-control comparison. We also coded whether the student, classroom, or school was used as the unit of analysis in the statistical procedures. Finally, we recorded the direction of the effect of summer school (positive or negative) and we calculated an effect size for each comparison. Along with the effect size, we recorded whether it was calculated from means and standard deviations or had to be estimated from inferential statistics.

## EFFECT SIZE METRIC

The effect size metric we used was the $d$-index, or standardized mean difference (Cohen, 1988). The $d$-index expresses the difference between two group means in terms of their common standard deviation.

Because the effects of summer school could be gauged in more than one way, the components of the $d$-index differed depending on the type of comparison. When the comparison involved a single sample of students tested before and after a summer program, the $d$-index was calculated by subtracting the postprogram mean score from the preprogram mean score and dividing this difference by the average of the preprogram and post-program standard deviations. When the comparison involved two samples of students, a sample that attended a summer program and a sample that did not (regardless of whether the groups were formed through random assignment), the $d$-index was calculated by subtracting the control group mean from the program group mean and dividing this difference by the average of the two group's standard deviations.

In both cases, a positive $d$-index indicated a positive effect of summer school. For example, a one-sample $d$-index equal to +.40 means that the sample's postprogram mean score was .40 standard deviations higher than its preprogram score. If a two-group $d$-index equals +.40 it means the group attending summer school scored .40 standard deviations higher than the nonattending group on the posttest.

Wherever possible, we calculated $d$-indexes from means and standard deviations provided by the report writers. When means and standard deviations were not provided but the values of the corresponding statistical tests of mean differences were given, we used formulas provided by Cooper (1998) to estimate $d$-indexes. Using the statistical tests to derive effect sizes introduced one important complexity into the meta-analysis. Specifically, some evaluations involving pretreatment versus posttreatment comparisons reported the outcomes of dependent $t$-tests and not the means and standard deviations at the time of the two tests. Therefore, these $d$-indexes relate to the variation in the amount of change experienced by each student, not the variation in raw test scores at each testing time. Thus, $d$-indexes derived from dependent $t$-test values should prove larger than those derived from raw means and standard deviations. As noted above, we coded how each $d$-index was derived and examined whether the derivation strategy was related to the magnitude of effect.

*Interpreting the magnitude of effect sizes.* No matter what the metric, effect size estimates are of limited value unless they are contrasted with other related effects of substantive interest. We cover the interpretation of effect sizes in detail in the discussion, but want to provide a general guide now for readers to use as they move through the results.

The first set of guidelines available to help place effect sizes in context also was provided by Cohen (1988). He proposed effect size values "to serve as operational definitions of the qualitative adjectives 'small,' 'medium,' and 'large'" (p. 12). Cohen recognized that judgments of "large" and "small" required a comparison between the effect under consideration and other contrasting ones. To define the adjectives "small" and "large," Cohen compared different magnitudes of effect "with a subjective average of effect sizes as are encountered in the behavioral sciences" (p. 13).

Cohen defined a small effect as $d = .20$, which he said was representative of personality, social, and clinical psychology research. A large effect was defined as $d = .80$ and was more likely to be found in sociology, economics, and experimental or physiological psychology. According to Cohen, then, an effect of summer school equal to, for example, $d = .20$ would be labeled "small" when compared to all the behavioral sciences, but about "average" when compared to other behavioral sciences closely aligned with education and child psychology.

## CODER RELIABILITY

After construction of the coding frame and its definitions, each relevant study was coded independently by two of the authors. All codes were then checked for consistency across the coders and disagreements were resolved in conference. Three authors regularly met during the coding and analysis process to discuss any codes about which coders felt it necessary to obtain additional input or confirmation from another. When coding was completed, most codes were rechecked before entry into the computer and during data analysis.

## SEARCH OUTCOMES

The literature search led us to 98 separate research reports that met the criteria for inclusion. Two reports, however, included the same data from a single program (Steinmiller & Duncan, 1991; Steinmiller & Steinmiller, 1993), so only one report was included in the data set. Another report contained cumulative data on 3 years of a program whose first 2 years were covered in two other reports (Sipe, 1986; Sipe, Grossman, & Milliner, 1987; Sipe, Grossman, & Milliner, 1988). The first two reports were omitted from the data set. Two additional reports described summer programs and conducted empirical evaluations but did not report the information we needed to code a trustworthy direction for the effect of the program. Smith (1972) and the Texas Education Agency (1982) evaluated the effects of multiple Title I programs, including remedial summer programs, and concluded that their overall impact had been positive. Neither evaluation, however, reported data in a way that permitted us to separate the effect of the summer program from other programs. Thus, a total of 93 reports were coded for inclusion in our data set.

The 93 reports included evaluations of 89 separate summer school programs. Several reports described the outcomes of evaluations of the same program during different years of operation. Specifically, five programs had multiple reports describing evaluations conducted in different years (Abram & Maurelli, 1980, after Abram & Cobb, 1979; Donaldson, 1992, after Donaldson, 1990, after Amorose, 1987; Petro et al., 1994, after Petro et al., 1993, after Rose et al., 1992; Rawson, 1993, after Rawson, 1992; Robbins & Thompson, 1991, after Robbins & Thompson, 1989). We coded these 12 reports as containing independent samples, even though they referred to the same program. Once, the same summer program was described and evaluated in more than one report, with separate reports describing data collected on different samples of students during the same year (Siegelman, 1975; Toledo, 1975).

Two reports included evaluations of two related summer programs during 2 consecutive years (Hanson, Yagi, & Williams, 1986, after Kashmuk & Yagi, 1985). Two other reports included evaluations of three related programs during 2 consecutive years (Kulieke, 1986, and Olszewski, Kulieke, & Willis, 1987). One report included data from 1 year of three separate summer programs (Kolloff & Moore, 1989). Another report (Klibanoff & Haggart, 1981) included evaluations of programs with two different goals.

Thirty-nine of the 93 reports included information on whether or not a summer program had a positive or negative effect on at least one academic-related outcome measure, but did not include enough information to calculate $d$-indexes for the effect. Fifty-four reports included enough information to calculate effect sizes. First, we examine the evaluations that provided only the direction of the effect.

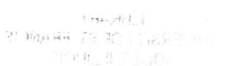

# III. NARRATIVE AND VOTE-COUNT SYNTHESIS OF COMPARISONS WITH ONLY DIRECTIONAL OUTCOMES

Effect sizes could not be derived from 39 reports, because the report included insufficient statistical data on pretest-posttest or control group comparisons. Most often, this was because information on the standard deviation of groups was missing and no information on the results of the pertinent inference test (i.e., $t$- or $F$-values) was provided.

Thirty of the 39 reports included evaluations of remedial programs, one contained an evaluation of a program for academic acceleration, and 10 included evaluations of programs with other or multiple goals. Forty-one evaluations appeared in the 39 reports, because two reports contained data on each of two related programs, one in the remedial goal category and one with multiple goals, evaluated in 2 consecutive years (Hanson, Yagi, & Williams,1986; Kashmuk & Yagi, 1985).

## PROGRAMS FOR REMEDIATION AND PROMOTION

Table 1 contains a description of the 30 reports, ordered by the year in which the report appeared, that included information on the direction of the effect of summer school when the goal of the program was to promote students who had failed a course or to remedy an academic deficiency. For each report, Table 1 presents the first author, year the report appeared, the state in which the evaluation was conducted, the number of students who took part in the evaluation, the grade level and any other defining student characteristics, the criteria for determining the success of the program, the subject matter of the outcome measures, and the number of individual samples revealing all positive (ap), mostly positive (mp), even (e), mostly negative (mn), and all negative (an) effects. These last determinations were made by examining all comparisons within an independent sample. For example, a sample that had four measures with two positive and two negative findings would be labeled "even (e)" and one with three positive and one negative finding "mostly positive (mp)."

TABLE 1

STUDIES OF REMEDIATION AND PROMOTION PROGRAMS PROVIDING ONLY DIRECTION OF OUTCOME

| Author | Year of Report | Location | Sample Size | Grade or Age | Student Characteristics | Type of Comparison | Outcome Measure | Direction of Results[1] |
|---|---|---|---|---|---|---|---|---|
| Godon | 1966 | California | 267 | 7th–9th | Below grade level | Pre-post | English, math, vocabulary, & spelling | 1 mp |
| Richardson | 1968 | California | 43 | 7th–9th | ? | Pre-post | Vocabulary & comprehension | 1 e<br>1 ap<br>1 an |
| Fox | 1969 | New York | 1,003 | 3rd–5th | Below grade level | ? | Reading | 1 e |
| Deling | 1972 | Michigan | ? | 3rd–4th | Migrant | Pre-post | English | 1 ap |
| Agnew | 1973 | ? | 150 | 2nd & 5th | Failing | Post-post | Vocabulary, comprehension, & communication | 2 e |
| Roderick | 1979 | Michigan | 23 | 1st–6th | Migrant | Post-post | Math & spelling | 1 ap |
| Dailey | 1979 | Colorado | 168 | 1st–10th | Migrant | Pre-post | Math & reading | 5 ap |
| Mangino | 1983 | Texas | 679 | 7th–8th | Failing | Post-post | Promotion | 2 ap |
| Pfeifer | 1985 | Oregon | 22 | 7th–8th | Failing | Post-post | English, math, science, geography, health, & world culture | 2 ap |
| Kashmuk | 1985 | Oregon | 129 | 3rd–7th | Failing | Pre-post | Math, reading, & language | 5 ap<br>2 mp<br>1 mn<br>1 an |
| Burnes | 1985 | Colorado | 2,055 | k–12th | Migrant | Pre-post | English, math, & communication | 1 e |

| Hansen | 1986 | Oregon | 225 | 3rd–7th | Failing | Pre-post | Math, reading, & language | 3 ap<br>4 mp<br>3 mn |
|---|---|---|---|---|---|---|---|---|
| Rachel | 1987 | Louisiana | 16,261 | 2nd–5th | Below grade level | Post-post | Retention | 4 an |
| Carroll | 1987 | Connecticut | 2,242 | k–8th | Below grade level | Pre-post | Math, reading, & language | 3 ap |
| Moss | 1986 | Utah | 761 | k–12th | Migrant | Pre-post | Math, reading, & spelling | 6 ap<br>2 mp |
| Moss | 1988 | Utah | 4,443 | k–12th | Migrant | Pre-post | Math, reading, & spelling | 1 ap |
| Trangmoe | 1988 | Montana | 330 | k–6th | Migrant | Pre-post | Math & reading | 27 ap |
| North Carolina | 1988 | North Carolina | 11,431 | 3rd–8th | Failing | Pre-post | CAT | 6 ap |
| Donaldson | 1989 | Ohio | 127 | 9th–12th | At risk | Pre-post | Math, reading, & language | 1 ap |
| McDaniel | 1989 | West Virginia | ? | 9th–10th | Below grade level | Pre-post | Math & reading | 1 ap |
| Donaldson | 1990 | Ohio | 123 | 9th–12th | Below grade level | Pre-post | Math, reading, & language | 1 ap |
| Taggert | 1991 | Utah | 109 | 3rd–8th | Migrant | Pre-post | Math & reading | 4 ap |
| New York | 1992 | New York | ? | 9th–12th | Underachieving | Pre-post | Writing | 1 ap |
| Rose | 1992 | Colorado | 2,343 | 2nd–12th | Migrant | Pre-post | Math & reading | 11 ap |
| Donaldson | 1992 | Ohio | 58 | 9th–12th | Below grade level | Pre-post | Math, reading, & language | 1 ap |
| Petro | 1993 | Colorado | 1,984 | 2nd–12th | Migrant | Pre-post | Math & reading | 2 ap |
| Petro | 1994 | Colorado | 1,069 | 2nd–10th | Migrant | Pre-post | Math & reading | 1 ap |
| Curry | 1996 | Texas | 172 | ? | Below reading level | Pre-post | Math & reading | 1 e<br>2 an |
| McNeeley | 1996 | Illinois | 175 | 3rd–6th | Below reading level | Pre-post | English | 2 ap |
| Ouellette | 1998 | Minnesota | 3,892 | 4th–6th | ? | Pre-post | Math & reading | 1 ap<br>5 ap |

[1]This column contains the number of independent samples revealing comparisons that were all positive (ap), mostly positive (mp), even (e), mostly negative (mn), and all negative (an).

The 30 reports of remedial programs included 121 separate independent samples generating 257 comparisons. Ninety-five of the independent samples produced results that showed positive effects of summer school on all comparisons and eight more samples were predominantly positive. Six samples showed neither predominantly positive nor negative effects of summer school. Eight independent samples produced all negative effects and four samples predominantly negative effects.

*Narrative description of predominantly negative evaluations.* Five reports produced all of the samples showing predominantly negative or all negative findings. In 1968, Richardson (1968) evaluated a summer school program in Oakland, California, designed to aid the language development of 7th, 8th, and 9th grade children of Spanish-speaking background. Specifically, the goal was to diminish students' deficiencies in reading by providing intensive language instruction. Language courses were infused with both English and Spanish in an effort to enrich students' appreciation of their heritage as well as provide remedial instruction in English. In addition to language instruction, students also took courses in mathematics, with electives in typing, art, homemaking, wood shop, and physical education. Three hundred and twenty students took part in the program. Pretest and posttest mean scores for the vocabulary, comprehension, and total reading batteries of the California Reading Test, however, were available on only 11 to 18 students, depending on the test. Eighth graders showed the most success, improving in both vocabulary and reading comprehension. Seventh graders showed a slight improvement in comprehension and a decline in vocabulary. Ninth graders declined in both vocabulary and comprehension. The authors reported that the standardized test scores were of "limited reliability" in evaluating the program, and that teachers reported improvements in skills, attitudes, and intergroup relations.

In a study by the Bureau of Evaluation in Louisiana (Rachel, 1987) the promotion and retention rates of 2nd through 5th grade students during the years 1980–1985 were examined. Data on summer school were collected at the state level for students participating in state-funded compensatory or remedial programs, so very limited information was provided on the individual summer school programs. Pretest data was collected on 1,623 2nd grade students during the spring of 1982, 4,288 3rd grade students during the spring of 1983, 3,729 4th grade students during the spring of 1984, and 6,621 5th grade students during the spring of 1985. Thus, it is likely that there was overlap from year to year in the students who constituted the samples. The retention rates of those students attending summer school were compared to the retention rates of students not attending a summer school. At each grade level, a greater percentage of compensatory education students who had attended summer school were retained than among compensatory education students who had not attended a summer school. Beyond their eligibility for compensatory education, however, no attempt was made to match students, so it is not clear what other factors (e.g., the severity of the learning deficiency) might have motivated a student's decision to attend summer school.

Curry et al. (1996) provided summary statistics for Title I summer programs conducted during the summer of 1995 in the Austin, Texas, school district. One hundred seventy-three kindergarten through 6th grade Title I students who had attended a summer program were compared with other Title I students. Summer school students in grades 5 and 6 showed higher standardized test scores in both reading and math than other Title I children, but students in grades 2 and 3 showed lower scores. Again however, no attempt was made to control for confounding factors that might have motivated some students to attend summer school and others not to attend.

Kashmuk and Yagi (1985) evaluated the 1983 and 1984 summer programs made available to students attending Portland, Oregon, schools. A variety of classes were provided including nonacademic (e.g., arts and crafts), and basic and remedial academic instruction. The authors did not break out results according to the type of class, but did report separate results for students labeled as "not promoted," "enrichment," or "gifted and talented." Based on these labels we assumed that students who were not promoted attended summer school for either remedial or promotion goals. A pre-post design was used to compare the change in achievement test scores in math, reading, and language usage for 3rd through 7th grade students who attended summer school. No significance tests were conducted and no standard deviations were reported. District average gain scores also were provided but no attempt was made to create a matched control. Most groups of "not promoted" summer school students showed losses on reading test scores but gains on math and language scores.

Hanson, Yagi, and Williams (1986) evaluated the same summer program in 1985. That year, the board of education decided to waive tuition for students who qualified for free or reduced-price lunch. The new policy nearly tripled the number of students attending summer school. This time, separate results were reported for students labeled as "not promoted," "remedial," "enrichment," or "gifted and talented." Of 30 comparisons involving students who attended summer school for remediation or to attain promotion to the next grade (5 grades × 2 student groups × 3 skill areas), 20 revealed a positive effect. However, 6 negative effects appeared among the 10 comparisons involving language usage, suggesting no positive effect for this skill area. Also, 8 of 15 effects involving students seeking grade promotion revealed smaller gains than the district as a whole.

A search for commonalities in the studies producing negative results reveals two features of research design that deserve mention. In two evaluations

31

(Curry et al., 1996; Rachel, 1987), the postprogram effect of summer school on participants was compared to other students who may not have been appropriate matches. Specifically, the control students could very plausibly have had higher achievement scores prior to the summer program. In the other three cases (Hanson, Yagi, & Williams, 1986; Kashmuk & Yagi, 1985; Richardson, 1968), negative results appeared predominantly on preprogram versus postprogram assessments of the reading and language skills of low SES summer school students. The summer learning loss literature suggests that this would be the crossing of an achievement domain and a student population in which positive pretest-posttest effects of summer program would be most difficult to demonstrate, because summer loss would be greatest without an intervention.

*A vote-count estimate of effect size.* Hedges and Olkin (1985) provided a technique by which the underlying magnitude of a treatment's effect can be obtained from the proportions of studies showing positive and negative directional effects. This approach requires that the vote counter know the direction of each test of the treatment and the sample size associated with each condition, treatment, and control. In addition, the procedure is dramatically simplified if the sample sizes of the treatment and control conditions are equal within studies and also across all tests of the treatment. The vote counter uses these values to enter a table, provided by Hedges and Olkin (1985), to find the estimated effect size.

Our directional database meets the first two, but not the third, requirement. For illustrative purposes and to give us a first estimate of what the effect size associated with summer school might be, however, we elected to employ the vote-count estimating procedure by using some assumptions to generate the "equal" sample sizes.

First, we had to devise an estimate for the "equal" sample sizes in our treatment and control conditions. Three of the 121 independent samples were missing data on sample size. Of the remaining 118, a total of about 75,400 students participated in the evaluations. The average total sample size in each independent sample was about 640, so equal samples in treatment and control conditions might be set at about 320. Because the data set contained a few evaluations with very large samples, however, the median total sample size was 35, or about 17 in each condition. Therefore, we decided to use both of these values to enter the tables.

Next, we had to calculate the proportion of results that were positive. Again, we decided to do this in two ways. First, we used as our proportion of positive results the number of independent samples that revealed all or predominantly positive findings ( $n = 103$ ) divided by all findings that were either positive or negative ( $n = 115$ ). This proportion was .896. Then, we entered the table using both the mean and median "equal" sample sizes within conditions. Using the mean sample size, the estimated effect size was $d = .10$. Using the median sample size the estimated effect size was $d = .44$. Then again, we used as our proportions of positive results the number of independent samples that had all positive findings ($n = 95$) divided by the number of findings that were either all positive or all negative findings ($n = 103$). This proportion was .922. Using the mean condition sample size the estimated $d$-value was $d = .12$. Using the median sample size the estimated $d$-value was $d = .49$. Thus, we could say that using the vote-count procedure to provide a very rough estimate of the effect of remedial and promotion summer programs suggested that participants scored between one tenth and one half of a standard deviation higher on the outcome measure than their preprogram scores or the scores of nonparticipants.

*Narrative descriptions of large evaluations.* There were nine evaluations of remedial or promotion summer programs that provided only directional outcomes but were based on samples of more than 1,000 students. We thought it might be informative to describe these studies.

Several of the large evaluations involved programs meant for migrant students. An evaluation of 15 migrant summer school programs conducted in 1983 and 1984 in Colorado collected data on 2,055 children in kindergarten through high school (Burnes, 1985). Instruction was available in languages other than English and an attempt was made to coordinate the delivery of other social services with the summer school program. Overall, positive gains in achievement test scores were made, with larger gains realized in math than in reading.

Migrant education programs in Colorado also were evaluated during the 1990s (Petro et al., 1993; Petro et al., 1994; Rose et al., 1992). Each year, over 1,000 students in grades 2 through 12 took part in the evaluations. Again, the results of testing math were positive, with somewhat more positive results for math than reading.

The Utah State Office of Education evaluated migrant education programs conducted at 10 schools during the summer of 1988 (Moss, 1988). One of the 10 programs was conducted during the regular school year as well as during the summer, with the remaining nine programs limited to the summer. The length of the programs was varied, with some programs lasting 28 days and others lasting 50 days. In addition to academic instruction, students were provided with other enriching experiences, including a study of culture, recreation, and self-actualization, as well as basic health services. Evaluation data provided by 404 students in grades kindergarten through 12 indicated that the summer programs had a positive impact on achievement with all student groups improving in reading, spelling, and mathematics. Thus, the large-scale evaluations of summer programs for migrant students revealed uniformly positive results and suggest that these programs often contain nonacademic components.

Carroll (1987) evaluated three years of 25 remedial summer programs throughout Connecticut for over 2,200 children in kindergarten through 8th grade. Children were identified for participation if they were involved in a Chapter 1 program and had attendance problems. Achievement gains in reading, math, and language arts were found.

Two large-scale studies focused on summer programs meant to assist students who had been retained in grade. First, North Carolina began administering a program for testing 3rd, 6th, and 8th graders' basic skills (North Carolina State Department of Public Instruction, 1988). Those students who scored below a criterion on the North Carolina Minimum Skills Diagnostic Tests and students who were retained in grade were invited to attend a basic education program in the summer. Students in all three grades (approximately 11,300 students in all) showed improvement in both 1986 and 1987. Second, the Louisiana evaluation conducted by Rachel (1987), and discussed above because of its negative results, included elementary school students who had been retained in grade. This was the only large-scale evaluation that produced equivocal results about the benefits of summer school.

Finally, Ouellette-Howitz and Murray (1998) evaluated the 1998 Minneapolis, Minnesota, Public Schools' summer session. Evaluation data were provided for approximately 3,900 3rd through 7th grade students. Students were evaluated with the standardized achievement tests in both reading and math during the school year and then again after summer school. Reading and math scores increased for all grades.

## PROGRAMS FOR ACCELERATION

We found only one report that evaluated a summer program with acceleration as a goal and that did not report enough data to calculate effect sizes. Lynch (1992) evaluated the impact of 6 years of a summer program meant to provide academically talented students, aged 12 to 16, an opportunity to complete high school courses in biology, chemistry, and physics. The program lasted 3 weeks and students stayed on a college campus. Students showed consistent achievement test score gains from pretest to posttest in biology. Participants entered the class with a score equivalent to the 25th percentile of a national high school junior and senior norm group. Posttest biology scores were at the 74th percentile. In chemistry, the average score moved from the 8th percentile to the 69th percentile. In physics, average percentiles changed from 34th to 70th. No standard deviations were reported for the test scores. Follow-up surveys indicated that program participants performed well in subsequent science classes. Thus, this study suggests positive experiences for participants.

## PROGRAMS WITH OTHER OR MULTIPLE GOALS

Table 2 contains a description of 10 reports that included information on the direction of the effect of summer school when the program had a goal that was not remediation or acceleration or when the evaluation examined a program with multiple goals and we could not obtain separate results by goal. In addition to the information given in Table 1, Table 2 also includes the goal(s) of the program.

The 10 reports included 45 separate independent samples generating 117 comparisons. Eighteen independent samples produced results that showed positive effects of summer school on all comparisons and 14 samples were predominantly positive. Five samples showed neither predominantly positive nor negative effects of summer school. Only one independent sample produced all negative effects and seven samples predominantly negative effects.

*Narrative descriptions of predominantly negative evaluations.* All of the independent samples that revealed negative effects of programs with other or multiple goals were contained in four reports.

Kashmuk and Yagi (1985), described above for their evaluation of Portland, Oregon, remedial summer programs, also presented data for students who attended summer school for enrichment purposes. Regular education children showed fairly consistent gains, although 4th graders declined in their reading scores and 6th and 7th graders declined in their language scores. Though gifted children showed consistent gains in reading and math, they showed consistent losses in language. The next year, Hanson et al. (1986) found that those students in summer school for enrichment gained most in pretest to posttest change in math but they lost most in reading and language. Similarly, gifted students showed gains in math and reading, but showed losses in language.

In Indianapolis, Indiana, the Marion County Public Library conducted a reading program that aimed to inspire children to a love of reading (Robbins & Thompson, 1991). Children who participated in the reading program were given control over what they read and how much they read. Incentives such as ice cream, pencils, and fast food were offered to children in an effort to encourage reading. The evaluation paid special attention to those children who were low achievers. One hundred sixty-four 1st through 6th grade students were evaluated for both vocabulary and reading comprehension. In general, students improved their vocabulary but

TABLE 2

Studies of Programs With Other or Multiple Goals Providing Only Direction of Outcome

| Author | Year of Report | Location | Goal | Sample Size | Grade or Age | Student Characteristics | Type of Comparison | Outcome Measure | Direction of Results[1] |
|---|---|---|---|---|---|---|---|---|---|
| Yinger | 1970 | Ohio | Other | 195 | post-7th | Volunteer | Post-post | General achievement | 1 ap |
| Martin | 1978 | ? | Prepare students for college | 138 | 9th–12th | Visually impaired | Pre-post | Student skills | 1 ap |
| Kashmuk | 1985 | Oregon | Enrichment | 430 | 3rd–6th | Volunteer/gifted | Pre-post | Math, reading, & language | 5 ap<br>9 mp<br>4 mn |
| Hansen | 1986 | Oregon | Enrichment | 491 | 3rd–7th | Volunteer/gifted | Pre-post | Math, reading, & language | 5 ap<br>3 mp<br>2 mn |
| Shapiro | 1986 | Louisiana | Drop-out prevention | 105 | 9th–12th | At risk | Post-post | Comprehension, computation, & concepts | 1 mp |
| Robbins | 1989 | Indiana | Increase positive attitudes | 132 | 1st–5th | At risk | Pre-post | Reading | 3 ap |
| Seever | 1991 | Missouri | Other | 865 | 6th–8th | ? | Pre-post | Math & reading | 1 mn |
| Robbins | 1991 | Indiana | Increase positive attitudes | 164 | 1st–6th | Below grade level | Pre-post | Vocabulary & comprehension | 1 ap<br>4 e<br>1 an |
| Smith | 1992 | Washington, DC | Enrichment | 406 | 6th | ? | Pre-post | General knowledge | 1 ap |
| Steinmiller | 1993 | Arkansas | Increase positive attitudes | ? | 9th–12th | ? | Pre-post | GPA | 1 ap<br>1 mp<br>1 e |

[1]This column contains the number of independent samples revealing comparisons that were all positive (ap), mostly positive (mp), even (e), mostly negative (mn), and all negative (an).

students' reading comprehension scores declined from pretest to posttest. Despite losses in comprehension, the authors noted that "overall, students in the study maintained their reading achievement levels over the summer period" (Robbins & Thompson, 1991, p. 19).

Seever (1991) evaluated the Kansas City, Missouri, summer school program that was implemented to provide remedial, developmental, and enrichment opportunities for kindergarten through 12th grade students. The summer school was conducted across five different sites, with one site offering a bilingual program. Seever concluded that there were "no sizeable differences between summer and spring testings" (1991, p. 2). Indeed, an evaluation involving 865 6th, 7th, and 8th grade students showed a decline from pretest to posttest in both math and reading scores.

*A vote-count estimate of effect size.* Three of the 45 independent samples were missing data on sample size. Of the remaining 42, about 2,900 students participated in the evaluations. Thus, the average total sample size in each independent sample was about 70, and equal samples in treatment and control conditions would be 35. Again, however, the data set contained a few evaluations with large samples, so the median total sample size was 35, or about 17 students in each condition.

We used here the same strategy to generate rough estimates of effect size that we used for programs with promotion or remedial goals. The proportion of predominantly positive findings ($n = 32$) divided by all findings that were either positive or negative ($n = 40$) was .80. Using the mean condition sample size, the estimated effect size was $d = .21$. Using the median sample size the estimated effect size was $d = .29$. The proportion of all positive findings ($n = 18$) divided by the number of findings that were either all positive or all negative ($n = 19$) was .947. Using the mean condition sample size the estimated $d$-value was $d = .40$. Using the median sample size, the estimated $d$-value was $d = .46$.

## SUMMARY

Despite their limitations, the studies that provided only directional information present clear evidence that summer school has positive effects on student achievement. Furthermore, by using some methods unique to meta-analysis, we were able to provide some rough quantitative estimates of what the magnitude of the summer school effect might be. Our ability to generate these estimates, however, should not be taken to mean that underreporting of research outcomes is not a serious problem. The most reliable and informative evaluations are those with precise descriptions of results. It is these studies that we turn to next.

# IV. META-ANALYTIC PROCEDURES USED ON COMPARISONS WITH KNOWN EFFECT SIZES

Fifty-four evaluation reports contained enough information to permit us to calculate effect sizes measuring the impact of summer school on at least one outcome measure. These comparisons were synthesized using meta-analytic techniques. First, we will detail the statistical procedures and conventions used in the meta-analysis. A schematic representation of how the methods of meta-analysis proceeded can be found in Figure 1. Next, a brief statistical overview of the set of comparisons will be given. Finally, we will describe the substantive results of the meta-analysis. In the course of this description, each of the 54 studies in the database will be described, with special attention paid to their unique features or findings.

## METHODS OF META-ANALYSIS

*Calculating average effect sizes.* In our coding procedures, we described how we calculated the standardized mean difference, or $d$-index, between summer school participants and the control condition. Having these estimates in hand, we used both weighted and unweighted procedures to calculate average effect sizes across all comparisons.

In the unweighted procedure, each effect size was given equal weight in calculating the average $d$-value. We also identified the median $d$-value. In the weighted procedure, each independent effect size was first multiplied by the inverse of its variance and the sum of these products was then divided by the sum of the inverses. The weighting procedure gives greater weight to effect sizes based on larger samples and is the generally preferred alternative. Variance estimates for one-group pretest-posttest $d$-indexes were based on the formula $v = (1 + (d^2/2))/n$. Variance estimates for two-group $d$-indexes were calculated using formulas given in Cooper (1998). When we calculated $d$-indexes associated with categories of moderator variables, we only calculated weighted averages.

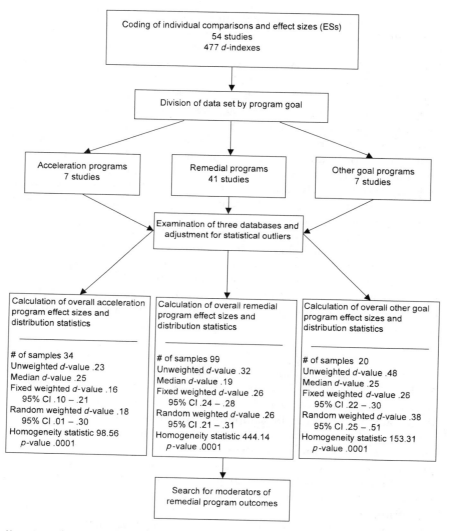

Note. One study contained evaluations of both remedial and other summer programs.

FIGURE 1.—Schematic diagram of the data analysis strategy and overall results

Also, 95% confidence intervals were calculated for weighted average $d$-indexes. If the confidence interval did not contain $d = 0$, then the null hypothesis of no summer school effect was rejected.

*Identifying independent hypothesis tests.* One problem that arises in calculating effect sizes involves deciding what constitutes an independent estimate of effect. Here, we used a shifting unit of analysis approach (Cooper, 1998). In this procedure, each effect size associated with a comparison is first coded as if it were an independent estimate of the treatment's impact. For example, if a single sample of students permitted comparisons of pre-program and postprogram math and reading scores, two separate $d$-indexes were calculated. For estimating the overall effect of summer school, how-ever, these two $d$-indexes were averaged prior to entry into the analysis, so that the sample only contributed one effect size. To calculate the overall weighted mean and confidence interval, this one effect size would be weighted by the inverse of its variance (based primarily on sample size, which should about be equal for the two component $d$-indexes). In an analysis that ex-amined the effect of summer school on math and reading scores sepa-rately, however, this sample would contribute one effect size to each estimate of a category mean effect size.

The shifting unit of analysis approach retains as much data as possible from each study, while holding to a minimum any violations of the assump-tion that data points are independent. Also, because effect sizes are weighted by sample size in the calculation of average $d$-indexes a study with many independent samples containing just a few students will not have a larger effect on average $d$-values than a study with only a single, or a few, large independent samples.

*Tests for moderators of effects.* Possible moderators of summer school ef-fects were tested using homogeneity analyses (Cooper & Hedges, 1994; Hedges & Olkin, 1985). Homogeneity analyses compare the amount of variance in an observed set of effect sizes with the amount of variance that would be expected by sampling error alone. The analyses can be carried out to determine whether (a) the variance in a group of indi-vidual effect sizes varies more than predicted by sampling error or (b) a group of average effect sizes varies more than predicted by sampling error. In the latter case, the strategy is analogous to testing for group mean differences in an analysis of variance or linear effects in a multiple regression.

Because it may be unfamiliar to some readers, we should explain the notation we used for presenting the results of homogeneity analyses. The homogeneity statistic itself is called $Q$ and it follows a chi-square distribu-tion. Therefore, we use the American Psychological Association format for reporting chi-square statistics (American Psychological Association, 1994). Before reporting the value of the $Q$-statistic, we present in parentheses the degrees of freedom associated with the test and the number of sam-ples, $k$, contributing to the analysis. This is followed by the value of the $Q$-statistic and its level of significance. Thus, the $Q$-statistic associated with a homogeneity analysis comparing two average $d$-values based on 99 samples and yielding an estimate of $Q = 3.84$ would be reported as follows:

$$Q(1, k = 99) = 3.84, \quad p < .05.$$

Such a result would indicate that the two group average effect sizes were not estimating the same underlying population value. We conducted the homogeneity analyses using programs we wrote ourselves in the Statistical Analysis System (SAS Institute, 1985).

*Fixed and random effects.* In addition to choosing an effect size metric, weighting procedures, and a unit for identifying independent comparisons, we also had to decide whether to conceptualize the effect of summer programs as fixed or random. An effect size is said to be fixed when the sampling error discussed above (that is, error solely due to participant differences) is viewed as the only random influence on effect-size estimates. Hedges and Vevea (1998) state that fixed-effect models of error are most appropriate when the meta-analyst "wishes to make inferences only about the effect size parameters in the set of studies that are observed (or a set of studies identical to the observed studies except for uncertainty associated with the sampling of subjects)" (p. 3).

It is also possible to view studies as containing other random influences. Specifically, summer school programs will differ in a multitude of ways, including differences in teachers, facilities, community economics, state regulations, and so on. These variations could lead us to view the programs in our meta-analysis as a random sample drawn from a (vaguely defined) population of all summer programs. If we believe that random variation in programs is a significant component of error, we must choose a statistical model that takes into account this study-level random variance in effect sizes.

It is rarely clear-cut which assumption, fixed or random, is most appropriate for a particular set of effect sizes. In practice, most meta-analysts opt for the fixed-effect assumption, because it is analytically easier to manage. Fixed-effects statistical models are often used, however, when random-effect models might be more appropriate. Indeed, a persuasive argument could be made that a random-effect model is most appropriate for the summer school literature. A random-effect model is indicated by (a) the large variation in summer program realizations and (b) our desire to draw inferences about all summer programs, not just those represented in our synthesis. Alternatively, it could be argued that a fixed-effect statistical model would be appropriate for our data if it is accompanied by a thorough search for moderators of effect sizes as part of the analytic strategy. Clearly, our strategy includes an exhaustive search for systematic moderating effects. Complicating matters further, evidence suggests that in the search for moderator variables, fixed-effect models seriously underestimate and random-effect models seriously overestimate error variance when their assumptions are violated (Overton, 1998).

Rather than opt for a single model that might be wrong, we chose to apply both models to our data. We conducted all our analyses twice, once employing fixed-effect assumptions and once random-effect assumptions. By employing this sensitivity analysis (Greenhouse & Iyengar, 1994), we could examine the effects of different assumptions on the outcomes of the synthesis. Differences in results based on which set of assumptions was used could then be part of our interpretation of results.

Also with regard to interpretation, there are two fine points about the relationship between fixed-effect and random-effect analyses that should be stated before we begin to examine our results. First, on occasion the homogeneity analyses comparing groups of effect sizes using fixed-effect and random-effect models produce identical $Q$-statistics. This occurs when the study-level variance component equals zero. In the vast majority of instances, the study-level variance component is greater than 0, and therefore the variance of random-effect estimates is larger and $Q$-statistics comparing average effect sizes are smaller. This is why random-effect homogeneity analyses tend to be more conservative than the corresponding fixed-effect results.

Second, instances occur in which the weighted average $d$-value for fixed-effect and random-effect models are noticeably different. Recall that weighted average $d$-values give greater weight to individual effect sizes that are based on larger samples or, equivalently, have smaller variances. When a random-effect analysis is carried out, a constant value, the study-level variance component, is added to each effect size's fixed-effect variance. Thus, the random-effect model tends to lessen the impact of sample size on the resulting weighted average $d$-value. This means that if the individual effect size magnitudes are related to sample size, the estimate of their average will change. When larger effect sizes are associated with smaller sample sizes, the random-effect weighted average $d$-values will be larger than the corresponding fixed-effect estimate. When larger effect sizes are associated with larger sample sizes (a rare occurrence), the random-effect weighted average $d$-values will be smaller than the corresponding fixed-effect estimate.

*Statistical adjustment for methodological outliers.* As is true for any data set composed of cases not under the control of the researcher, we confronted the possibility that significant correlation could exist among some of our moderator variables. For example, evaluations that used pretest-posttest change scores also might be more likely to sample students from economically disadvantaged backgrounds. The confounding of methodological, student, program, and outcome characteristics highlights the fact that plausible rival hypotheses will exist whenever a claim is made for a causal link between the effect of a summer program and one of the moderating variables.

Of course, under the circumstances that prevail in research synthesis, rival hypotheses always exist and causal claims are tenuous at best. Assertions about causality based on synthesis-generated evidence should always be taken as suggestive only (see Cooper, 1998, for a discussion of differences between study-generated and synthesis-generated evidence). When we have cases known to have correlated predictors, however, we can use statistical techniques to control for some rival hypotheses. For example, we can use multiple regression procedures to adjust each $d$-value so as to remove variation correlated with different methodological factors. Then, analyses can be run that examine student, program, and outcome moderators using both the unadjusted and adjusted $d$-index as the predicted variable. If a substantive characteristic still proves to be a significant moderator of summer school effects, we can be more confident this relation is not the spurious result of a confound with a methodological variation.

We chose to employ this strategy in our analyses. As was true of our decision to examine the data using both fixed-effect and random-effect models, the use of two estimates of effect permitted us to interpret our findings under both liberal and conservative assumptions.

In sum then, the test of each substantive moderator was conducted four times. The four analyses represent a full crossing of fixed-effect and random-effect models with unadjusted $d$-indexes and $d$-indexes adjusted to remove all variance associated with methodological factors.

## OVERVIEW OF COMPARISONS IN THE META-ANALYTIC DATABASE

The 54 reports from which $d$-indexes could be obtained described 52 separate summer school programs. Six reports presented evaluations of three programs conducted in separate years (Abram & Maurelli, 1980, after Abram & Cobb, 1979; Olszewski et al., 1987, after Kulieke, 1986; Rawson, 1993, after Rawson, 1992). Two reports presented data from separate students in the same program (Siegelman, 1975; Toledo, 1975). Offsetting these multiple reports about the same programs were two sets of two reports that included data on three separate programs each (Olszewski et al., 1987, after Kulieke, 1986; Kolloff & Moore, 1989). The 54 reports included 153 independent samples. Most evaluations contributed between one and four independent samples, but three studies contributed 6, 8, and 15 samples.

A total of 477 comparisons were made between students before and after attending summer school or between students who did and did not attend summer school. The smallest number of comparisons conducted within any independent sample was one, occurring in 59 samples. The largest number of comparisons was 16, occurring within three separate samples collected for one study (Leviton, 1973) and a single sample in another study (Curry, 1990). The sample sizes for comparisons ranged from 6 to 2,808. About 33,500 students participated in all.

Documents appeared between the years 1963 and 1995. The median year of document appearance was 1981. Twenty-six of the reports were internal evaluations, 12 were dissertations, nine of the reports appeared as journal articles, two were evaluations conducted by a private research firm, two were evaluations conducted by university research centers, and one each appeared as a master's thesis, in a book, or as an ERIC document with no other identification.

*Program goals.* We found no program with the stated goal of preventing juvenile delinquency. Thirty-seven of the documents described programs that had as a goal the remediation of learning deficiencies. Three studies evaluated programs meant solely to prevent at-risk high school students from dropping-out (Curry, 1990; Opuni, Tullis, & Sanchez, 1990; Wells, Springer, & McCready, 1987) or to prevent "culturally deprived" kindergartners from falling behind in first grade (Wasik & Sibley, 1969). Because of the low frequency of prevention program evaluations and because of the similarity in samples and content of these programs and remedial programs, we combined these two sets of evaluations together, bringing the total number of studies in the remediation category to 41 and the total number of independent samples in this category to 99.

The remaining 13 studies, accounting for 54 independent samples, were divided among programs with the goal of acceleration (7 studies, 34 samples), and programs with other or multiple goals (6 studies, 15 samples). One evaluation (Klibanoff & Haggart, 1981) included independent samples drawn from both remedial and multiple-goal (five samples) summer programs.

Because of substantial differences in study characteristics, we decided to examine separately the evaluations of programs with the three different goals. The main meta-analysis relates to programs with the goal of remediation of learning deficiencies.

# V. META-ANALYTIC AND NARRATIVE SYNTHESIS OF PROGRAMS FOR REMEDIATION OF LEARNING DEFICIENCIES

## DESCRIPTION OF THE DATABASE

As noted above, the 41 studies of remedial summer programs for which we could generate effect sizes included 99 independent samples of students. Approximately 26,500 students were included in all the samples combined. The number of independent samples in each evaluation ranged from 1 to 10. A total of 385 comparisons were made in studies of remedial summer programs.

Table 3 includes some critical characteristics of each of the 41 studies. It provides the first author of each report, the year of the report and the year of the program (in parentheses), the location of the program, the number of students included in the data analysis, the grade level and achievement label of the students in summer school, the type of comparison group, the content of the outcome measures, and the range of $d$-values provided by the independent samples (with the number of independent samples in parentheses).

An examination of frequency distributions for the coded variables revealed several characteristics for which little or no variation was discernible across the studies or samples. Methodologically, all studies used the student as the unit of statistical analysis. All studies had a pretest and all posttests were identical to the pretest or were an alternate form of the same pretest. Only one study used a cohort design. When participants were equated in nonequivalent-group designs, nearly all studies did so by matching students rather than by statistical control. With regard to program characteristics, nearly all programs employed experienced teachers as instructors. No report included an overall dropout rate for the program and very few reports included the number of students in the entire summer school program, or the exact day on which the summer program ended.

Because of a lack of variation, the above characteristics could not be examined as potential moderators of the outcomes of evaluations. The lack

TABLE 3

MEAN EFFECT SIZE BY INDEPENDENT SAMPLE FOR REMEDIAL AS THE GOAL

| First Author | Year of Report (Program) | Location | Number of Students in Analyses | Grade | Achievement Label | Type of Comparison | Outcome Measure | $d$-Index Range ($k$) |
|---|---|---|---|---|---|---|---|---|
| Fox | 1967 (1967) | New York, NY | 818 | 6th–8th | Failing | Pre-post | Math & reading | .17 to .37 (2) |
| Garofalo | 1968 (1968) | Central NY | 49 | k–6th | ? | Pre-post | Math & reading | .98 (1) |
| Geis | 1968 (1967) | Suburban Los Angeles, CA | 33 | 1st | At risk | Post-post and pre-post | Reading | .15 (1) |
| Gousha | 1968 (1968) | Milwaukee, WI | 360 | 1st–6th | Failing | Pre-post | Math & reading | .23 to .29 (3) |
| Fox | 1969 (1969) | New York, NY | 206 | 3rd & 5th | Below grade level | Pre-post | Reading | −.13 to −.08 (2) |
| Wasik | 1969 (1968) | Durham, NC | 16 | k | At risk | Pre-post | Math, reading, full & verbal IQ | .48 to .66 (2) |
| Cramer | 1969 (1966) | West Alexander, OH | 103 | 4th–8th | Below grade level | Pre-post | Reading | 1.50 to 1.50 (5) |
| Baxley | 1971 | Eloy, AZ | 8 | k–2nd | Failing | Pre-post | Math & reading | 1.45 (1) |
| Culp | 1973 (1972) | IN city | 226 | 3rd | Below grade level | Post-post and pre-post | Math & reading | −.22 to −.08 (2) |
| Leviton | 1973 | Suburban, MN | 60 | 1st–3rd | Learning disabled | Post-post and pre-post | Attitudes, math, & reading | .10 to .64 (3) |
| David | 1974 (1971) | Four cities | 137 | k–1st | At risk | Post-post and pre-post | Math, reading, & sounds | .12 to .79 (4) |
| Bergeth | 1975 (1975) | Minneapolis, MN | 123 | 3rd–4th | Underachieving | Pre-post | Reading | .03 (1) |
| Siegelman | 1975 (1975) | New York, NY | 2835 | 9th–10th | Below grade level | Pre-post | Math | .36 to .42 (2) |

| Study | Year (pub) | Location | N | Grade | Population | Design | Subject | Effect size |
|---|---|---|---|---|---|---|---|---|
| Toledo | 1975 (1975) | New York, NY | 2808 | 9th | Below grade level | Pre-post | Reading | .06(1) |
| Woloshin | 1975 (1975) | New York, NY | 904 | 9th–10th | Below grade level | Pre-post | Reading | .43 to .47(2) |
| Williams | 1977 (1976) | East Feliciana Parish, LA | 163 | 4th | Below grade level | Post-post and pre-post | Reading | .11 to .30(2) |
| Womble | 1977 (1975) | ? | 2352 | 4th & 8th | ? | Post-post and pre-post | Math & reading | −.17 to .12(4) |
| Abram | 1979 (1978) | Daviess County, KY | 490 | 1st–7th | Below grade level | Post-post and pre-post | Math & reading | .10 to .19(2) |
| Doss | 1979 (1978) | Austin, TX | 170 | 2nd–5th | ? | Post-post and pre-post | Reading | .15 to .19(3) |
| Abram | 1980 (1979) | Daviess County, KY | 307 | 1st–7th | Below grade level | Post-post | Math & reading | −.13 to .87(6) |
| Porterfield | 1980 (1980) | Austin, TX | 317 | 7th–8th | Below grade level | Pre-post | Math & reading | .24 to .36(2) |
| Klibanoff | 1981 | National | 1303 | 2nd–6th | Underachieving | Pre-post | Math & reading | −.07 to .24(10) |
| Menousek | 1983 | Midwestern city | 64 | k–12th | Other disability | Post-post | Self-help skills | −.13(1) |
| Fonzi | 1984 (1982) | Dade County, FL | 2081 | 3rd & 5th | Learning disabled | Post-post | Math & reading | −.24 to .67(8) |
| Amorose | 1987 (1987) | Columbus, OH | 137 | 8th–12th | At risk | Pre-post | Math & reading | .50(1) |
| Franklin | 1987 | Chicago, IL | 55 | 1st–7th | Other disability | Post-post | Math & reading | .15(1) |
| Merkel-Keller | 1987 (1985) | Five urban districts in NJ | 80 | 10th | Below grade level | Pre-post | Math, reading, & writing | .16(1) |
| Miller | 1987 (1986) | New York, NY | 1625 | 1st–6th | Mild handicap | Pre-post | Math & reading | .37 to .50(4) |

*continued*

TABLE 3 *continued*

| First Author | Year of Report (Program) | Location | Number of Students in Analyses | Grade | Achievement Label | Type of Comparison | Outcome Measure | d-Index Range (k) |
|---|---|---|---|---|---|---|---|---|
| Sipe | 1988 (1987) | Five large urban cities | 5549 | 9th–10th | Below grade level | Post-post and pre-post | Math & reading | .01 to .10 (2) |
| Tam | 1987 (1987) | Columbus, OH | 26 | 2nd | Below grade level | Pre-post | Reading | .74 (1) |
| Wells | 1987 | Northern LA | 80 | 7th–10th | At risk | Pre-post | Math & reading | .77 (1) |
| Hyman | 1988 (1987) | SC | 149 | 4th–8th | Failing | Pre-post | Attitudes, math, & reading | .11 to .55 (5) |
| Ward | 1989 (1986) | NC | 471 | 3rd & 6th | Failing | Post-post | Absences, CAT, math, & reading | –.16 to .03 (2) |
| Cobb | 1990 | | 39 | 2nd–6th | Learning disabled | Pre-post | Reading | .41 (1) |
| Curry | 1990 (1989) | Four parishes in LA | 90 | 8th–9th | ? | Post-post and pre-post | Math, reading, & self-esteem | .29 (1) |
| Opuni | 1990 (1990) | Houston, TX | 178 | 5th–9th | Failing | Pre-post | Attitudes | .11 (1) |
| Welch | 1990 (1989) | Metropolitan school district | 185 | 6th–8th | Failing | Post-post and pre-post | Writing | 1.50 (1) |
| Brown | 1991 (1990) | Pawley's Island, SC | 274 | Adolescent age | At risk | Pre-post | Reading & attitudes about achievement | .31 to .48 (3) |
| Rawson | 1992 | Lexington, IN | 42 | 4th–6th | At risk | Pre-post | Attitudes | .19 (1) |
| Rawson | 1993 | Lexington, IN | 116 | 3rd & 5th | Academically disadvantaged | Pre-post | Math & reading | .19 to .31 (2) |
| D'Agostino | 1995 (1992) | Chicago, IL | 1496 | 5th | At risk | Post-post and pre-post | Reading | .08 (1) |

NOTE. The number of students in analyses is the sum of independent sample sizes. *k* equals the number of independent samples in the evaluation report.

of variation also places limits on the generalizability of findings. For example, we would have to exercise great caution and provide a clear rationale if we proposed that the results of the meta-analysis were generalizable to programs using inexperienced teachers.

For several other codes, we found sufficient variation to permit analysis but certain categories within the coding had to be combined. About 45% of all samples took part in internal evaluations, whereas the rest were scattered among the other categories. Therefore, we collapsed this variable into internal evaluations versus all others, labeled external evaluations.

With regard to program participants, samples described as low income were compared to samples described as middle class, with samples of students from varied economic backgrounds or for which no economic information was given excluded from the analysis. As might be expected, we found no evaluation of a remedial program that described the students' achievement level as "gifted" or "average." Evaluators described 24 samples as containing students "at-risk," 31 samples as "underachievers or below grade level," 26 samples as "failing or retained," and 18 samples as "learning disabled or otherwise impaired."

Programs evaluated in their 1st year of operation were compared to all programs evaluated after more than 1 year of operation. Samples drawn in large urban areas were compared to samples drawn from rural, suburban or small urban communities combined, with mixed and unknown community samples dropped from this analysis. Samples that were identified as comprised of volunteer students were compared to samples of nonvolunteers combined with samples for which we could not discern the sample's volunteer status.

About half (53%) of evaluations explicitly described the content of the summer curriculum and only three categories of content were used. Curricula were described as either specific to reading (9%), containing both a reading or language and a math component (16%), or including numerous, varied subject matters (27%).

About one third of all posttest measures were administered immediately following the end of summer classes, but another third were given in September or October of the year following summer school. About one sixth had longer delays, and these were combined into one category. About one sixth of the reports did not mention when the posttest was given. The metric of the outcome measures was grouped into raw scores (85%) and all types of norm-referenced scales.

Finally, the coding of the subject matter of the outcome measures revealed about half of all measures were specific to reading and/or language arts and about 40% to mathematics. We found no measures specific to other subject areas. About 2% of measures related to general academic or intellectual abilities, and 6% to nonacademic areas such as attitudes toward school, self-esteem, and study habits.

## DISTRIBUTION AND MEASURES OF CENTRAL TENDENCY

*Adjustment of statistical outliers and extreme values.* First, we inspected the distribution of the 385 $d$-indexes using a stem-and-leaf plot. Applying Tukey's (1977) definition, we identified three positive $d$-index values that qualified as statistical outliers, that is, $d$-values that were more than three interquartile ranges beyond the 75th percentile. We discovered that these three $d$-values ($d$ = 4.40, 2.75, 2.71) came from two studies.

The single largest effect size came from an evaluation of a video-assisted intervention meant to improve the writing skills of students who had failed at least two courses during the previous school year (Welch & Jensen, 1990). Teachers were instructed in how to support the videos and implementation of the instructional model was monitored throughout a 6-week session. The evaluators used both pretreatment versus posttreatment comparisons and posttest comparisons of treated and control students to assess the effect of the program. Both the students' knowledge of paragraph structure and student writing samples served as outcome measures. The pre-to-post comparison on the knowledge test revealed a $d$-index of 4.40. The report suggested that the content of the videos and the knowledge test was very closely aligned.

The second and third largest $d$-values came from a single evaluation. Cramer and Dorsey (1969) published a report on a summer reading program for poor-performing students in grades 4 through 8. This program also included a parent-involvement requirement (parents had to attend two conferences), had to overcome the added obstacles of serving a rural community where farm chores were a typical part of children's summer routines, and had to provide transportation to and from school. The program involved small classes of 15 students with individualized instruction and met for 5 weeks, five times a week, for 3 hours each day. Results revealed improved reading scores among participants as well as improvements in attitudes toward school, although data on attitudes were not included in the report.

As the descriptions suggest, these two studies had several unique characteristics that were potentially desirable and of substantive interest but that appeared only infrequently in other programs. In fact, these studies might provide examples of "best practice." Therefore, we chose not to remove their comparisons from our data set. Instead, we decided to Winsorize the three outliers along with 10 other comparisons that had $d$-values greater than 1.5. All 13 adjusted comparisons (3.4% of all comparisons) were set to a value of $d = 1.50$ and were included in all subsequent analyses. In this manner, no single effect size could have an overly large influence on any analysis (especially those analyses in which only a few comparisons might appear), but at the same time we would not lose the potentially important information contained in them (Barnett & Lewis, 1978). In addition to the evaluations by Welch and Jensen (1990) and Cramer and Dorsey (1969; which included five $d$-values greater than 1.5), four other studies revealed unusually large effect sizes (Baxley & Hinton, 1971; David, 1974; Leviton, 1973; Tam, 1987).

In a similar manner, we also examined the distribution of sample sizes to look for extreme values. Six independent samples appearing in three evaluations were based on sample sizes that met the Tukey (1977) criteria for identification as statistical outliers.

Siegelman (1975) prepared an evaluation of a summer mathematics program for Title I students attending New York City public schools. In addition to instruction in basic math skills, the program was meant to help ease the transition between junior high and high school by having students take classes in their new school and meet the new school staff. The 9th grade sample ($n = 1,850$) revealed a $d$-value of .42, and the 10th grade sample ($n = 985$) revealed a $d$-value of .36 on the Metropolitan Achievement Test. During the same year, Toledo (1975) evaluated a New York City program meant to improve reading skills conducted simultaneously with Siegelman (1975). The goals and sites of the reading program were identical to the math program, but neither report makes mention of the other component, so we coded these evaluations as independent samples from the same program. Toledo reported a positive program effect of $d = .06$.

Sipe, Grossman, and Milliner (1988) provided an evaluation of the Summer Training and Education Program (STEP). STEP was designed to increase basic skills and lower drop-out rates and teen pregnancy among disadvantaged and poor-achieving 14- and 15-year-olds by providing basic academic skills and life skills instruction, and work experiences for two consecutive summers. One program component required at least 80 hours of part-time work provided by the federally funded Summer Youth Employment and Training Program. Support for the model development and pilot-testing were provided by both private foundations and public agencies. The programs ran in five urban areas: Boston, Fresno, Portland (Oregon), San Diego, and Seattle. Both pretest-posttest and participant-versus-nonparticipant comparisons were provided for samples that ranged in size from 877 to 1,876. The authors reported large learning losses over summer for control group students and lesser losses for program participants. Only rough $p$-levels (i.e., $p < .10$, .05, and .01) and differences in means, however, were provided without standard deviations. Therefore, $d$-values had to be estimated using sample sizes and $p$-levels. All the summer program effects were positive for treatment versus control comparisons, but some were not significant. Thus, the estimated values ranged from $d = .01$ to $d = .15$.

In addition to the six unusually large samples contained in the above three studies, we decided to Winsorize 14 other sample sizes greater than 500. We set these values to 500, and also set all treatment and control sample sizes (when these were known) to a maximum value of 250. We adopted these procedures because sample sizes are used to calculate the weights applied to each effect size when weighted averages are calculated. By restricting the weightings in this manner, we ensured that no single sample could have an exceptionally large influence on the outcome of an analysis. In addition to the Siegelman (1975), Toledo (1975), and Sipe, Grossman, and Milliner (1988) studies, three other evaluations included samples whose size was adjusted (D'Agostino & Hiestand, 1995; Fonzi, 1984; Woloshin, 1975).

In the context of sample size, we should also mention an evaluation reported by Klibanoff and Haggart (1981), even though the individual sample sizes did not undergo adjustment. This evaluation was part of the large-scale study of the sustaining effects of compensatory education on basic skills. Data were collected on as many as 120,000 students in a nationally representative sample of elementary schools. Data on preprogram and post-program reading and math scores were presented for 15 cohorts of students, 10 in remedial summer programs, attending 1st through 5th grade. Sample sizes ranged from 53 to 190. Because this evaluation encompassed many schools and therefore many programs, little specific information was provided on the content of the summer programs. The sample effect sizes in this evaluation ranged from $d = -.07$ to $d = .24$.

*Measures of central tendency and dispersion* (see Figure 1). After Winsorizing the effect sizes, the average unweighted $d$-value for the 385 comparisons was $d = .28$. Using the 99 independent samples as the unit of analysis, the average unweighted $d$-value was $d = .32$. The median effect size was $d = .19$. When the 99 independent effect sizes were weighted by the inverse of their variance the average $d$-index was $d = .26$. Thus, making no distinctions among effects based on research methodology or program, student, or outcome characteristics, the average student outcome score after remedial summer school was over one quarter of a standard deviation higher than the average student score before summer school or without summer school. The 95% confidence interval for the weighted $d$-index under the assumption of a fixed program effect encompassed a lower value of $d = .24$ and an upper value of $d = .28$. Under the assumption that summer programs were a random effect, the confidence interval expanded to a lower value of $d = .21$ and an upper value of $d = .31$. Therefore, the null hypothesis that remedial summer school had no effect on students clearly can be rejected.

Table 4 presents a stem-and-leaf display of the *d*-indexes before being Winsorized. The stems list the first two digits of each effect size value and the leaves list the hundredths value for each effect size. For example, the +.7 row of Table 4 indicates that there were four *d*-indexes with values of .71, .74, .77, and .79. Taken as a whole, Table 4 reveals that 86 of the 99 *d*-values showed remedial summer school to have a positive effect. The 13 negative effects appeared in eight different evaluations, but in only three cases did the negative findings represent a majority of findings for independent samples within the evaluation. We will now take a closer look at these three evaluations.

Fox and others (1969) described a summer school program carried out for New York City elementary school students from disadvantaged neighborhoods. The programs had multiple components, but the evaluation focused on a component meant to improve the reading skills of children reading below grade level. Because the program was broad-based,

TABLE 4

STEM AND LEAF DISPLAY OF REMEDIAL SUMMER SCHOOL EFFECT SIZES

| Stem | Leaf |
|------|------|
| +2.7 | 15 |
| +2.3 | 7 |
| +2.0 | 7 |
| +1.9 | |
| +1.8 | 7 |
| +1.7 | |
| +1.6 | 7 |
| +1.5 | |
| +1.4 | 5 |
| +.9 | 8 |
| +.8 | 7 |
| +.7 | 1479 |
| +.6 | 467 |
| +.5 | 0057 |
| +.4 | 0122234788 |
| +.3 | 011446677 |
| +.2 | 23446899 |
| +.1 | 00001111224455555566778899999 |
| +.0 | 12233568889 |
| −.0 | 57788 |
| −.1 | 333367 |
| −.2 | 24 |

NOTE. Effect sizes are based on independent samples ($n = 99$).

encompassing 153 schools, little precise information was given on the components of the program. Using a pretest-posttest design, Fox reported lower reading scores in fall than in spring for both 3rd graders, $d = -.08$, and 5th graders, $d = -.13$.

Culp (1973) evaluated a summer program in reading and math for Indiana inner-city elementary school students who were performing approximately 1 year below grade level. Participants' postprogram scores were compared to unmatched controls. Mostly negative comparisons for summer school on achievement were found, with slightly greater negative comparisons for math, $d = -.22$, than reading, $d = -.17$. The author cautioned that the two groups were dissimilar on the pretests and no attempt at matching was made.

Menousek (1983) assessed summer programs for special education students who had severe mental handicaps. The programs were carried out in four school districts and program content and design varied from district to district but tended to be based on students' specific needs. The dependent variable was the child's level of self-sufficient behavior, including toileting, personal hygiene, eating, dressing, and/or home-living skills. Results were mixed across outcome measures but on average indicated poorer performance on the part of summer program attendees, $d = -.13$. Students who attended summer school, however, were compared to other handicapped students who did not and, beyond the shared handicap, no attempt was made at matching of participant and control groups. We might conclude, then, that the three studies that produced uniformly negative appraisals of summer school were also among the poorest in research design.

The fixed-effect test for homogeneity of effect sizes indicated we should reject the hypothesis that the $d$-indexes were all estimating the same underlying population value, $Q(98, k = 99) = 444.14$, $p < .0001$, or, put differently, we should reject the hypothesis that sampling error alone was responsible for variation in $d$-values. Therefore, it was most appropriate for us to look for characteristics of evaluations and programs that moderate the effect size estimates. First, we examined potential moderators related to research methodology, followed by student characteristics, the context in which the program was delivered (e.g., type of community, size of the program), features of the program, and characteristics of the achievement measures.

## TESTS FOR METHODOLOGICAL MODERATORS OF EVALUATION OUTCOMES

Table 5 presents the fixed-effect and random-effect $Q$-statistic along with the mean $d$-values and the variation around the mean $d$-value that

TABLE 5

Methodological Moderators of Remedial Summer School
Evaluation Outcomes

| Moderator | $k$ | Fixed | | | Random | | |
|---|---|---|---|---|---|---|---|
| | | $Q$ | $d$ | +/−ci | $Q$ | $d$ | +/−ci |
| Type of control | 125 | 35.93* | | | 8.74* | | |
| pretest-posttest | 81 | | .24 | .02 | | .30 | .06 |
| posttest-posttest | 44 | | .07 | .05 | | .09 | .07 |
| How was pre-post $d$ derived? | 81 | 84.91* | | | 0.66 | | |
| means & $SD$s | 65 | | .19 | .02 | | .27 | .07 |
| dependent $t$ | 16 | | .40 | .04 | | .40 | .08 |
| Type of two-group design | 44 | 1.78 | | | 0.88 | | |
| random assignment | 11 | | .14 | .11 | | .14 | .11 |
| nonequivalent group | 33 | | .05 | .06 | | .08 | .09 |
| Was NE control matched? | 33 | 0.00 | | | 0.00 | | |
| no | 9 | | .06 | .12 | | .07 | .21 |
| yes | 24 | | .05 | .07 | | .08 | .09 |
| What was matched variable? | 24 | 3.94* | | | 3.03 | | |
| academic achievement | 17 | | .11 | .09 | | .14 | .13 |
| all others | 7 | | −.03 | .11 | | −.03 | .11 |
| Who did evaluation? | 99 | 38.11* | | | 0.01 | | |
| externals | 55 | | .16 | .04 | | .25 | .08 |
| internals | 44 | | .30 | .03 | | .28 | .07 |
| Number of students in analyses | 109 | 2.27 | | | 2.27 | | |
| <90 | 55 | | .27 | .05 | | .38 | .11 |
| >90 | 54 | | .24 | .03 | | .19 | .06 |
| Was implementation monitored? | 99 | 37.96* | | | 1.03 | | |
| no[1] | 73 | | .20 | .03 | | .23 | .06 |
| yes | 26 | | .34 | .04 | | .33 | .09 |
| Was attendance monitored? | 99 | 14.52* | | | 0.79 | | |
| no[1] | 63 | | .22 | .03 | | .24 | .06 |
| yes | 36 | | .29 | .03 | | .29 | .09 |
| Were nonattendees dropped? | 99 | 8.67* | | | 0.37 | | |
| no[1] | 72 | | .24 | .02 | | .27 | .06 |
| yes | 27 | | .31 | .04 | | .23 | .10 |

Note. NE = nonequivalent group
[1]Includes samples from reports that did not mention this moderator.
*$p$ < .05.

encompasses the 95% confidence interval for the different levels of each methodological moderator. For example, if an average "Fixed $d$" equals .20 and its associated "+/−ci" equals .05, it means that the 95% confidence interval for the average value is .15 to .25. The reader also might note that if the $d$-value in the table is larger than the "+/−ci" then the $d$-value is significantly different from $d = 0$ at $p < .05$. Thus, even when differences between levels of a moderator variable are not significant, most $d$-indexes associated with different levels of moderators do indicate significantly positive effects of summer school.

*Type of control group.* The first moderator we examined concerned the type of control group used in the evaluation. First, we compared the size of the $d$-indexes in samples that used as the comparison pretest scores of students who attended summer school versus samples that used posttest scores from either nonequivalent groups or randomly assigned groups of students who did not attend summer school. The fixed-effect homogeneity analyses revealed that the type of control comparison was a strong predictor of effect size, $Q(1, k = 125) = 35.93$, $p < .0001$. The average $d$-index for one-group pretest-posttest designs was $d = .24$, but for two-group designs $d = .07$. (The number of samples exceeds 99 because a single independent sample could contribute more than one data point to this analysis if it contained both types of comparisons. This also was possible for a few other moderators described below). The random-effects analysis also found the type of control group to be significantly associated with variance in $d$-values, $Q(1, k = 125) = 8.74$, $p < .005$. The random-effects average $d$-index for one-group pretest-posttest designs was $d = .30$, but for two-group designs $d = .09$.

*Derivation of d-value.* Within the pretest-posttest designs, we next compared $d$-values that were derived from means and standard deviations with $d$-values derived from dependent $t$-tests. The fixed-effect model revealed significant differences between the derivation strategies, $Q(1, k = 81) = 84.91$, $p < .0001$, suggesting larger effects were calculated using dependent $t$-tests, $d = .40$, than using means and standard deviations, $d = .19$. The random-effect model revealed no significant difference, $Q(1, k = 81) = 0.66$, *ns.*

*Type of two-group design.* Next, within the two-group designs we compared samples from evaluations that employed random assignment of students to conditions with designs that used nonequivalent (designated NE in Table 5) or intact groups. Both the fixed-effect homogeneity analysis, $Q(1, k = 44) = 1.78$, *ns,* and the random-effect homogeneity analysis revealed nonsignificant difference, $Q(1, k = 44) = 0.88$, *ns.* The average $d$-index for samples that employed random assignment was $d = .14$, however, and this effect was significantly different from zero using either model of error. For nonequivalent-group designs, the average effect was $d = .05$ under fixed-effect assumptions and $d = .08$ under random-effect assumptions, and neither model led to a rejection of the null hypothesis.

Because studies that employ random assignment are considered most trustworthy, we next examined in more detail the five evaluations that used this design feature. Geis (1968) conducted the first evaluation of a summer program that randomly assigned students to treatment and control conditions. A summer program in reading was provided for students entering 1st grade in a district serving predominantly middle-class families. The students had been identified as at-risk for reading failure. The program included a parent-involvement component that required parents to attend (a) a preprogram conference at which the eligibility of their child was discussed, (b) a 2-hr summer session, (c) a conference during the program at which related reading activities to be carried out at home were discussed, and (d) a group discussion at the end of the program. Classroom instruction was carried out in small groups of five or six students. The results revealed the summer program had a positive effect on two standardized reading test scores when treatment and control students were compared both in September of the following year, $d = .64$, and 9 months later, $d = .44$. Interestingly, a comparison of preprogram and September scores using only program participants revealed a drop in scores ($d = -.62$), suggesting the major benefit of the program may have been to prevent even greater summer loss.

Leviton (1973) examined a summer program involving both reading and math instruction for 1st, 2nd, and 3rd grade students with learning disabilities who lived in an upper-middle-class suburb. The sample sizes were small, including 26, 22, and 16 students for 1st, 2nd, and 3rd grade, respectively. Each child received individualized attention in groups of no more than three students. Random assignment was used to pick program participants from students nominated by teachers. Measures of achievement and self-concept were taken both immediately after the summer program and with a delay of 6 months. Based on significance tests, the researcher concluded that little evidence was found for both the immediate and delayed effectiveness of summer school. Contrary to Geis (1968), the average effect size for preprogram versus postprogram scores of participants was quite large ($d = .81$), whereas the postprogram comparison of participants and controls was small ($d = .08$) and negative at the time of the delayed measurement ($d = -.08$).

The Summer Projects Study was designed to assess the effects of several Follow Through summer programs meant to improve achievement for low-income children in kindergarten or 1st grade (David, 1974). Students were selected based on parent interest. Originally, Follow Through programs in 11 cities were chosen to take part in the evaluations, but 7 cities were discarded primarily due to problems in accomplishing random assignment. Four cities (Kansas City, Missouri, Tuskegee, Alabama, Uvalde, Texas, and Chattanooga, Tennessee) provided the needed data. Treatment groups contained between 19 and 28 students and control groups between 6 and 23 students. The author raised concerns about (a) preprogram differences among groups that suggested random assignment was suspect in the Kansas

City sample and (b) differences in parent and administrative reports of students who did and did not attend the program. Statistical analyses adjusted for some of these concerns. The four sites produced evidence of positive summer school effects but the estimates varied dramatically. Again, the postprogram scores of participants were considerably higher than their preprogram scores, $d = .74$, but the postprogram comparison of the students randomly assigned to participant and control conditions also revealed a positive effect for summer school, $d = .31$.

The evaluation of the STEP program described above because of the size of its samples also included random assignment of students to treatment and control conditions (Sipe, Grossman, & Millner, 1988). All of the estimated effects of summer school based on comparisons of participating and control students were positive.

Curry (1990) reported an evaluation of a 7-week residential program conducted at Nichols State University. The program provided remedial education, job training, and counseling, and was designed to prevent dropping out among 30 at-risk 8th graders identified by their teachers as at-risk. Four measures, reading achievement, math achievement, self-esteem, and locus of control, were taken. During the program, participants made gains in all areas but control-group students showed declines. A 6-month follow-up revealed the treated students maintained the gains they evidenced at the end of the program. The overall effect of the treatment was $d = .29$.

*Matching procedures.* The results comparing one-group and two-group designs and comparing random assignment and nonequivalent-group designs suggested that interventions using nonequivalent groups had the smallest estimates of the effect of summer school. One explanation for this finding might be that these studies chose control students who were poorly matched with summer school participants. More precisely, the intact control groups might have contained samples of students who were achieving at higher levels relative to treated students prior to summer school and this difference might have suppressed the estimate of the positive effect of summer school.

To test this possibility, we next examined whether, among nonequivalent-group designs, samples that were chosen using some attempt to match students revealed different effects from samples that were not matched. The homogeneity analyses revealed that the use of matching procedures was not associated with a significant amount of variance in effects whether a fixed-effect, $Q(1, k = 33) = 0.00$, *ns*, or random-effects model was used, $Q(1, k = 33) = 0.00$, *ns*. Within studies that used matching, however, the average $d$-index in samples that employed academic achievement as the matching variable revealed larger fixed-effect $d$-values, $d = .11$, than did samples that used any other matching procedures, $d = -.03$, $Q(1, k = 24) =$

3.94, $p < .05$. This effect was nearly significant under random-effect assumptions, $Q(1, k = 24) = 3.03$, $p < .09$.

*Evaluation agent.* Next, we examined whether evaluation reports prepared by the same organization that implemented the summer program contained different results from reports prepared by outside agents. Using a fixed-effect model, we found reports that were prepared by the school or school district also responsible for delivering the program reported larger effects, $d = .30$, than evaluations prepared by external agents, $d = .16$, $Q(1, k = 99) = 38.11$, $p < .0001$. Using a random-effect model, the comparison was not significant, $Q(1, k = 99) = 0.01$, *ns*, probably because of a large increase in the random-effect estimate of the $d$-index for external evaluations, $d = .25$.

*Size of the evaluation.* The next methodological moderator we looked at concerned the size of the evaluation. Under both fixed- and random-effect assumptions, we found no significant relationship between the number of students who provided data for the evaluation and the magnitude of the summer school effect, for fixed and random models, $Q(1, k = 109) = 2.27$, *ns*.

*Indicators of treatment fidelity.* Another homogeneity analysis revealed significant fixed-effect difference between samples in evaluation reports that stated the implementation of the summer school program was monitored, $d = .34$, and reports that made no mention of including such a procedure, $d = .20$, $Q(1, k = 99) = 37.96$, $p < .0001$. The random-effects model showed no significant difference between evaluations with and without monitoring of implementation, $Q(1, k = 99) = 1.03$, *ns*.

*Student attendance.* Similarly, fixed-effect differences were found between samples from reports with information on student attendance, $d = .29$, and reports that made no mention of measuring student attendance, $d = .22$, $Q(1, k = 99) = 14.52$, $p < .0001$, but random-effects estimates were not significantly different, $Q(1, k = 99) = 0.79$, *ns*. And again, fixed-effect homogeneity analyses showed that evaluations in which students were dropped from the data set if they did not meet a minimum attendance criterion reported larger $d$-values, $d = .31$, than reports that made no mention of employing this technique, $d = .24$, $Q(1, k = 99) = 8.67$, $p < .005$, but not the random-effects analysis, $Q(1, k = 99) = 0.37$, *ns*.

*Adjustment for methodological confounds.* In order to create $d$-index estimates that were uncorrelated with methodological variation, we decided to control for seven features of evaluation design and analysis. These features were (a) one-group pretest-posttest versus two-group designs, (b) how the $d$-index was derived, (c) whether the evaluation report was prepared internally or by an external agent, (d) the number of students in the sample, (e) whether the treatment implementation was monitored, (f) whether attendance was monitored, and (g) whether nonattendees were dropped from the analyses. The three remaining methodological characteristics examined as moderators but not included in the adjustment (type of two-group control, matching, and matched variables) were left out because a large majority of evaluations had no values on these variables.

The unit of analysis used for purposes of adjusting $d$-values was the individual comparison or effect size ($n = 385$). The seven variables were entered into the regression equation simultaneously. The residuals from the regression were then used in the moderator analyses described below but, because the residuals have an average value of zero, we first added .28, the average of the unweighted $d$-values based on the 385 comparisons, to each residual. This is a procedure that is called "fitting an average value to the regression."

## TESTS FOR STUDENT CHARACTERISTICS THAT MODERATE EVALUATION OUTCOMES

Five student characteristics were tested as moderators of the effects of summer school. The results of these analyses are displayed in Table 6.

*Grade level.* Under fixed-effect assumptions, both the lowest grade level of students who took part in the summer program, $Q(1,k = 96) = 8.61$, $p < .005$, and the highest grade level, $Q(1,k = 96) = 10.31$, $p < .005$, were positively related to the magnitude of the program's effect. This effect held true also for adjusted $d$-values, for lowest grade, $Q(1,k = 96) = 78.47$, $p < .0001$, for highest grade, $Q(1,k = 96) = 64.03$, $p < .0001$. Under random-effect assumptions, the relationship between grade level and summer program effects was not significant, for unadjusted $d$-values lowest grade, $Q(1,k = 96) = 0.09$, *ns*, unadjusted $d$-values highest grade, $Q(1,k = 96) = 0.07$, *ns*, for adjusted $d$-values lowest grade, $Q(1,k = 96) = 2.31$, *ns*, adjusted $d$-values highest grade, $Q(1,k = 96) = 1.34$, *ns*.

We examined the mean $d$-indexes related to grade-levels in three groups roughly encompassing early primary grades, late primary grades, and secondary grades. We noticed evidence of a curvilinear relationship, suggesting summer programs were most effective for the youngest and oldest students. Table 6 reveals that the largest effect sizes were associated with summer programs that served more advanced students, with $d$-values from both fixed-effect and random-effect models ranging from .29 to .36. In all cases, students in middle grades revealed the smallest effect sizes, with $d$-values ranging from .14 to .21. Students in the lowest grades fell between the two extremes, with $d$-values ranging from .19 to .32. Because of this pattern, we

## TABLE 6

### Student Moderators of Remedial Summer School Evaluation Outcomes

| Moderator | k | Unadjusted d-indexes | | | | | | Adjusted d-indexes | | | | | |
|---|---|---|---|---|---|---|---|---|---|---|---|---|---|
| | | Fixed | | | Random | | | Fixed | | | Random | | |
| | | Q | d | +/-ci | Q | d | +/-ci | Q | d | +/-ci | Q | d | +/-ci |
| Lowest Grade | 96 | 8.61* | | | 0.09 | | | 78.47* | | | 2.31 | | |
| k–2 | 29 | | .31 | .05 | | .32 | .10 | | .20 | .05 | | .20 | .05 |
| 3–4 | 39 | | .14 | .04 | | .14 | .07 | | .15 | .03 | | .19 | .07 |
| 5–8 | 28 | | .31 | .03 | | .35 | .09 | | .35 | .03 | | .36 | .08 |
| Highest Grade | 96 | 10.31* | | | 0.07 | | | 64.03* | | | 1.34 | | |
| k–3 | 32 | | .24 | .05 | | .24 | .09 | | .19 | .05 | | .22 | .07 |
| 4–6 | 35 | | .19 | .04 | | .21 | .10 | | .17 | .04 | | .19 | .07 |
| 7–12 | 29 | | .29 | .03 | | .31 | .09 | | .35 | .03 | | .34 | .09 |
| Sex of Sample | 19 | 0.16 | | | 0.16 | | | 2.81 | | | 0.22 | | |
| females | 8 | | .13 | .13 | | .13 | .13 | | .38 | .13 | | .32 | .21 |
| males | 11 | | .10 | .09 | | .10 | .09 | | .24 | .09 | | .23 | .11 |
| SES | 48 | 7.02* | | | 3.83 | | | 4.38* | | | 4.38* | | |
| low | 42 | | .23 | .03 | | .20 | .07 | | .24 | .03 | | .20 | .06 |
| middle | 6 | | .56 | .24 | | .46 | .41 | | .49 | .24 | | .44 | .31 |
| Achievement Label | 99 | 22.01* | | | 0.62 | | | 49.72* | | | 3.92 | | |
| failing | 26 | | .23 | .04 | | .25 | .09 | | .21 | .04 | | .23 | .07 |
| disability | 18 | | .34 | .05 | | .27 | .11 | | .23 | .05 | | .25 | .07 |
| underachieving | 31 | | .27 | .04 | | .29 | .11 | | .36 | .03 | | .36 | .11 |
| at-risk | 24 | | .19 | .04 | | .23 | .09 | | .19 | .04 | | .20 | .08 |

*$p < .05$.

conducted homogeneity analyses to determine the significance of any curvilinear relation. We found significant curvilinear relations for all fixed-effect tests, for lowest grade unadjusted $d$-values, $Q(1,k = 96) = 31.92$, $p < .001$, for highest grade unadjusted $d$-values, $Q(1,k = 96) = 9.78$, $p < .005$, for lowest grade adjusted $d$-values, $Q(1,k = 96) = 102.84$, $p < .0001$, for highest grade adjusted $d$-values, $Q(1,k = 96) = 18.12$, $p < .0001$. One significant and one near significant curvilinear effect was found in the analyses using random-effect assumptions, for lowest grade unadjusted $d$-values, $Q(1,k = 96) = 2.77$, $p < .10$, for highest grade unadjusted $d$-values, $Q(1,k = 96) = 0.19$, $ns$, for lowest grade adjusted $d$-values, $Q(1,k = 96) = 4.05$, $p < .05$, for highest grade adjusted $d$-values, $Q(1,k = 96) = 0.31$, $ns$.

*Student sex.* The sex of the student proved to be a nonsignificant moderator of $d$-values, regardless of whether fixed or random models were used with unadjusted or adjusted $d$-values, for fixed-effect unadjusted $d$-values, $Q(1,k = 19) = 0.16$, $ns$, for random-effect unadjusted $d$-values, $Q(1,k = 19) = 0.16$, $ns$, for fixed-effect adjusted $d$-values, $Q(1,k = 19) = 2.81$, $ns$, for random-effect adjusted $d$-values, $Q(1,k = 19) = 0.22$, $ns$. Six studies that examined the effect of summer school on males and females separately contributed 16 independent samples to this analysis (with the remaining three samples coming from studies that contained only males). Because of their within-study comparisons, these evaluations deserve a closer examination.

Wasik and Sibley (1969) evaluated a summer program for culturally disadvantaged students entering 1st grade. The program used token reinforcement and isolation techniques to teach a wide array of carefully delineated academic skills. Preprogram to postprogram changes in standardized intelligence test scores showed a dramatic effect and the effect was larger for males, $d = .66$, than for females, $d = .48$.

Williams (1977) also conducted a study that looked at the student's sex as a moderator of a program's effect. This evaluation assessed the impact of a summer program meant to improve the reading ability of 4th grade students who were in a remedial reading class. A nonequivalent-group comparison was used. In general, no significant differences were found between students who did and did not attend the program, although there was some evidence that females in the summer school program, $d = .30$, outperformed males in the program, $d = .11$.

Abram and Cobb (1979) and Abram and Maurelli (1980) examined 2 successive years of the effects of a summer program in Owensboro, Kentucky. Analyses considering the sex of the student revealed results that did not replicate from one summer to the next. In 1979, the program had a slightly larger effect on females, $d = .19$, than on males, $d = .10$, but in 1980 two of three comparisons showed larger effects for males.

Finally, the evaluations mentioned earlier by Culp (1973) and Sipe, Grossman, and Milliner (1988) both included single comparisons favoring females. Thus, as with the overall outcome of the homogeneity analysis, the comparisons of males and females within the same evaluations suggested no consistent pattern of sex differences in the effectiveness of summer school.

*Socioeconomic status.* The socioeconomic background of students in the sample proved related to evaluation outcomes under all testing conditions, for fixed-effect unadjusted $d$-values, $Q(1, k = 48) = 7.02$, $p < .01$, for random-effect unadjusted $d$-values, $Q(1, k = 48) = 3.83$, $p < .051$, for fixed-effect adjusted $d$-values, $Q(1, k = 48) = 4.38$, $p < .04$, for random-effect adjusted $d$-values, $Q(1, k = 48) = 4.38$, $p < .04$. Across the four analyses, the estimated $d$-values ranged from .20 to .24 for low SES samples and from .44 to .56 for middle SES samples, a sizeable difference in effect.

Given the robustness of the SES effect, it might be informative to examine the programs that involved samples at the most extreme points on the SES scale. Three evaluations that sampled middle-class students have already been mentioned. Welch and Jensen (1990) was described because it contained the largest of all effect sizes. Its contribution to this analysis was $d = 1.50$. Geis (1968), with an average $d$-value equal to $d = .15$, and Leviton (1973), with three $d$-values equal to .64, .10, and .40, were described because they used random assignment procedures. In all three cases, the evaluation included only middle-class samples.

The remaining middle-class sample came from Doss et al. (1979). These authors reported an evaluation of a summer program focusing on both remediation and enrichment activities for Title I, migrant, and fee-paying (middle-class) students in the Austin, Texas, school district. Comparisons of participants and matched controls revealed the program had no significant long-term effects on students' achievement. The $d$-index for Title I students was $d = -.05$, for migrant students, $d = .06$, and for fee-paying students, $d = -.02$. When preprogram and postprogram scores were compared, however, there was evidence of substantial gain (for Title I students, $d = .51$, for migrant students, $d = .86$, and for fee-paying students, $d = .71$). The evaluators recommended that sufficient time and resources needed to be budgeted for careful and complete planning of summer school and that a number of small and diverse programs rather than one large and homogeneous program be implemented and evaluated.

On the other end of the economic spectrum, children of migrant workers probably represent students who suffer the greatest economic disadvantage. In addition to Doss et al. (1979), who sampled from three economic groups, Garofalo (1968) presented an evaluation of a summer

63

program meant to improve the reading and math abilities and the self-concept, social skills, and health and nutrition habits of children of migrant workers in upstate New York. Standardized testing revealed positive effects. Parent questionnaires revealed little involvement with their child's summer school experience. Twenty-three percent of the parents felt the summer school had a negative effect on their child and 10% saw the effect as positive, whereas two thirds "hoped" it was positive. Teachers praised the flexibility of the program and its opportunities for individualized instruction. This program revealed a large pretest-posttest difference of $d = 0.98$.

Baxley and Hinton (1971) reported an evaluation of a summer program that targeted language instruction for children of migrant workers attending school in Eloy, Arizona. The program included preservice and inservice training for teachers. In the program, children received meals and engaged in recreational activities as well as language instruction in an experiential setting. Data on only eight students, a random sample of 15% of students in the program, revealed a $d$-value of 1.64, which was adjusted to 1.50 for use in this analysis.

In sum then, there is robust evidence from the meta-analysis that summer programs have larger positive effects on middle-class than low-income students. The effect of summer school, however, was positive and greater than zero for both economic groups. Furthermore, evaluations of programs with children of migrant workers, though few in number, also suggest large effects of summer programs.

*Achievement label.* The final student characteristic we examined as a moderator of the effect of summer school was the achievement label given to the participating students. Although all student groups showed significant gains associated with attending summer school, fixed-effects models revealed significant differences between students given different achievement labels. Curiously however, with unadjusted $d$-values, the means suggested that students labeled as learning-disabled or physically or mental impaired appeared to benefit more from summer school, $d = .34$, than students labeled underachieving, $d = .27$, failing, $d = .23$, or at-risk, $d = .19$, $Q(3, k = 99) = 22.01$, $p < .0001$. After adjustment for methodological confounds, students labeled as underachieving, $d = .36$, revealed the largest effect size, whereas $d$-values for students labeled with learning disabilities, $d = .23$, or as failing, $d = .21$, or at-risk, $d = .19$, varied little amongst themselves, $Q(3, k = 99) = 49.72$, $p < .0001$. Although nonsignificant, the analyses using random-effect assumptions were consistent with this latter finding, for unadjusted $d$-values, $Q(31, k = 99) = 0.62$, *ns*, for adjusted $d$-values, $Q(3, k = 99) = 3.92$, *ns*.

Conventional wisdom suggests that students with disabilities should benefit considerably from summer school because it may prevent dramatic summer losses. This supposition is reflected in federal law that mandates summer services for many students eligible for special education. Because of this, we examined more closely evaluations of programs for children with special needs.

The 18 independent samples of students with learning disabilities were drawn from six separate summer programs. Fonzi (1984) examined a summer program for 3rd and 5th grade students with learning disabilities. Eight samples varied in size from 98 to 510. Some students attended the summer program part-time and some full-time, depending on their individual educational prescription. Instruction was given in basic skills in a resource room for part of the day and the remainder of the day was spent in a regular classroom. The evaluation used the statewide testing battery in math and communications (reading and writing) as the outcome measure. Students who attended summer school performed better than their counterparts who did not attend, but the effect was not consistent across all grade levels. The $d$-values ranged from $d = -.24$ to .67. Also, Fonzi broke out the results of the summer school program according to reading and mathematics stanines. This permitted us to examine the effects of summer school for students with different levels of learning deficiency. Students in the four samples who scored in the lowest stanines (1–3) revealed summer school effects of $d = -.13, -.07, .18,$ and .18. Students in the highest stanines (4–6) showed summer school effects of $d = -.24, .22, .57,$ and .67. Thus, within this study there was great variation in effects, but students with the less severe learning deficiencies appeared to benefit most from summer school.

Miller, Berney, and Mulkey (1987) evaluated a New York City summer program that incorporated athletics with instruction in reading and mathematics. The emphasis in instruction was on a holistic approach using the students' experiences with sports to teach language arts. Math instruction focused on word problems and practical skills. Individual instructional plans were developed for students who were described as mildly to moderately handicapped. Positive effects were found, with $d$-values ranging from .37 to .50.

Franklin (1987) assessed a summer program for students with severe emotional disturbances. Forty-five students attending the program were compared to 10 matched students not attending the program. The outcome measures were change scores from before to after the program on reading comprehension and reading recognition. Program attendees outperformed nonattendees on comprehension, $d = .33$, but did worse on recognition, $d = -.03$.

Cobb, Bonds, Peach, and Kennedy (1990) evaluated an intensive 6-week reading program for elementary school students with learning disabilities or behavior disorders. The program used a phonics approach and measured students' preprogram and postprogram auditory and visual discrimination skills. A positive program effect, $d = .41$, was found, with 22 of 39 students showing improvement.

Menousek (1983), mentioned earlier for having revealed a negative effect, assessed a summer program for students who had severe mental handicaps. The dependent variable was the child's level of self-sufficient behavior, and results were mixed across outcome measures but on average indicated poorer performance on the part of summer program attendees, $d = -.13$.

The study by Leviton (1973) has twice been mentioned, because it employed random assignment and a middle-class sample. We noted earlier that among the comparisons based on random assignment this evaluation produced small effects of summer school, although all were positive.

The programs for students with learning disabilities are largely positive in outcome. Examination of the effect sizes revealed by the individual studies suggest no unique characteristics of these studies or findings that might distinguish them from students sampled from other populations of students. A possible, although highly speculative, suggestion is that programs for students with more severe disabilities tended to show smaller effects than programs for students with milder disabilities.


## TESTS FOR PROGRAM CONTEXT MODERATORS
## OF EVALUATION OUTCOMES

Five program context features were tested as moderators of the effects of summer school. The results of these analyses are displayed in Table 7.

*Year of evaluation and number of years the program had run.* The year in which the program was evaluated revealed no significant relation to program outcomes, for fixed-effect unadjusted $d$-values, $Q(1,k = 99) = 0.15$, *ns*, for random-effect unadjusted $d$-values, $Q(1,k = 99) = 0.15$, *ns*, for fixed-effect adjusted $d$-values, $Q(1,k = 99) = 3.35$, $p < .07$, for random-effect adjusted $d$-values, $Q(1,k = 99) = 1.90$, *ns*. The number of years the program had been in existence revealed one significant effect. When fixed-effect assumptions were used and $d$-values were adjusted to remove correlation with methodological factors, programs evaluated in their first year, $d = .29$, had larger effects than programs evaluated in later years, $d = .23$, $Q(1,k = 99) = 8.31$, $p < .005$. No other analysis of the year of the program came close to producing a significant effect, for fixed-effect unadjusted $d$-values, $Q(1,k = 99) = 0.15$, *ns*, for random-effect unadjusted $d$-values, $Q(1,k = 99) = 0.15$, *ns*, for random-effect adjusted $d$-values, $Q(1,k = 99) = 0.23$, *ns*.

## TABLE 7
### Program Context Moderators of Remedial Summer School Evaluation Outcomes

| Moderator | k | Unadjusted d-indexes | | | | | | Adjusted d-indexes | | | | | |
|---|---|---|---|---|---|---|---|---|---|---|---|---|---|
| | | Fixed | | | Random | | | Fixed | | | Random | | |
| | | Q | d | +/-ci | Q | d | +/-ci | Q | d | +/-ci | Q | d | +/-ci |
| Year of Evaluation | 99 | 0.15 | | | 0.15 | | | 3.35 | | | 1.90 | | |
| prior to 1976 | 36 | | .28 | .03 | | .33 | .10 | | .33 | .03 | | .33 | .10 |
| 1976–1981 | 25 | | .13 | .05 | | .13 | .05 | | .13 | .05 | | .13 | .05 |
| 1982 or after | 38 | | .30 | .04 | | .28 | .08 | | .26 | .03 | | .28 | .07 |
| Years in Existence | 99 | 0.15 | | | 0.15 | | | 8.31* | | | 0.23 | | |
| 1 year[1] | 69 | | .26 | .03 | | .31 | .07 | | .29 | .03 | | .27 | .07 |
| >1 year | 30 | | .25 | .03 | | .19 | .07 | | .23 | .03 | | .24 | .05 |
| Type of Community | 73 | 11.27* | | | 4.97* | | | 3.26 | | | 3.26 | | |
| other | 34 | | .38 | .05 | | .44 | .12 | | .34 | .05 | | .41 | .10 |
| large urban | 39 | | .28 | .03 | | .24 | .07 | | .29 | .03 | | .26 | .08 |
| Number of Schools | 50 | 54.94* | | | 5.75* | | | 8.27* | | | 1.22 | | |
| <8 | 26 | | .37 | .05 | | .48 | .14 | | .37 | .05 | | .45 | .16 |
| >8 | 24 | | .26 | .03 | | .21 | .09 | | .26 | .03 | | .24 | .07 |
| Number of Classes | 21 | 40.21* | | | 2.13 | | | 13.37* | | | 1.34 | | |
| <8 | 11 | | .64 | .13 | | .90 | .36 | | .42 | .13 | | .67 | .35 |
| >8 | 10 | | .18 | .05 | | .13 | .12 | | .17 | .05 | | .16 | .10 |

[1]Includes samples from reports that did not mention this moderator.

*p < .05.

*Type of community.* The type of community in which the program operated was a strong predictor of summer school outcomes, revealing significant effects under both fixed and random assumptions with unadjusted *d*-values and near-significant effects with adjusted *d*-values, for fixed-effect unadjusted *d*-values, $Q(1,k=73) = 11.27$, $p < .001$, for random-effect unadjusted *d*-values, $Q(1,k = 73) = 4.97$, $p < .03$, for fixed-effect adjusted *d*-values, $Q(1,k=73) = 3.26$, $p < .08$, for random-effect adjusted *d*-values, $Q(1,k = 73) = 3.26$, $p < .08$. Summer programs conducted in rural communities, suburbs, or small cities revealed substantially larger *d*-values, with estimates ranging from .34 to .44, than programs carried out in large cities, ranging from .24 to .29, although these programs also had significant positive effects.

*Number of schools and classes.* Two indicators of the size of summer programs, the number of schools and classrooms encompassed by the program, also suggested a relation with program outcomes, but here the effects were largely confined to analyses using the fixed-effect models. Programs that generally used fewer schools revealed larger effects than programs occupying more schools, for fixed-effect unadjusted *d*-values, $Q(1,k=50) = 54.94$, $p < .0001$, for random-effect unadjusted *d*-values, $Q(1,k=50) = 5.75$, $p < .02$, for fixed-effect adjusted *d*-values, $Q(1,k=50) = 8.27$, $p < .005$, for random-effect adjusted *d*-values, $Q(1,k = 50) = 1.22$, *ns*. A median split showed that summer programs conducted in less than eight schools had larger *d*-values, ranging from .37 to .48, than programs conducted in eight or more schools, ranging from .21 to .26. Programs that used fewer classrooms also revealed larger effects under fixed-effect assumptions than programs employing a greater number of classrooms, for fixed-effect unadjusted *d*-values, $Q(1,k=21) = 40.21$, $p < .0001$, for random-effect unadjusted *d*-values, $Q(1,k = 21) = 2.13$, *ns*, for fixed-effect adjusted *d*-values, $Q(1,k = 21) = 13.37$, $p < .0005$, for random-effect adjusted *d*-values, $Q(1,k=21) = 1.34$, *ns*. A median split showed that summer programs conducted with less than eight classrooms had larger *d*-values, ranging from .42 to .90, than programs conducted with eight or more classrooms, ranging from .13 to .18.

Both of the moderators related to the size of a program suggested that larger effects were associated with smaller summer programs. Earlier, we pointed out that another indicator of program size, the actual number of students who were in the program, was reported too infrequently to test as a moderator of program outcomes. Only 11 of the 41 reports included information on the size of the entire summer program and most of the remaining programs could not confidently be assumed to be large or small. Of the 11 reports, 5 reports said the program served less than 200 students and 4 said it served more than 1,000 students. It might be instructive to examine these latter four evaluations.

Bergeth (1975) reported on the Minneapolis Public Schools Title I summer school program. The program served approximately 3,000 students and was aimed at students showing the greatest academic need. Reading assessments were carried out on 3rd and 4th graders from 16 different schools by comparing preprogram and postprogram test scores. A positive effect of the summer program on reading was found, $d = .03$.

Womble (1977) evaluated a summer program for disadvantaged youth with about 1,200 participants and found no effect on standardized achievement test scores when summer program students were compared to non-participants. Interestingly, the staff of the summer program changed at midsession with no coordination of effort. The four $d$-indexes from this evaluation ranged from $d = -.17$ to .12.

In addition to Bergeth (1975) and Womble (1977), the studies by Siegelman (1975) and Toledo (1975) concerning a summer program in New York City reported participant populations in excess of 8,500 students. These evaluations reported effect sizes of $d = .42$, .36, and .06.

Examining the $d$-values in the four reports of large-scale summer program suggests that their average effects were below those of the average effect for all evaluations. This finding, together with the findings on the number of schools and classrooms, and on urban versus other communities, reveals a fairly consistent pattern suggesting larger effects for smaller programs.

## TESTS FOR PROGRAM FEATURE MODERATORS OF EVALUATION OUTCOMES

Seven program features were tested as moderators of the effects of summer school. The results of these analyses are displayed in Table 8.

*Volunteers.* Whether or not the evaluation report stated that students attended summer school on a voluntary basis proved a significant moderator of $d$-values under fixed-effect assumptions, for fixed effect unadjusted $d$-values, $Q(1, k = 99) = 50.06$, $p < .0001$, for random-effect unadjusted $d$-values, $Q(1, k = 99) = 5.14$, $p < .03$. Programs that were voluntary were associated with smaller effects of summer school, $d = .09$ and .10, respectively, than programs that were nonvoluntary or gave no relevant information, $d = .29$ and .30. After adjustment for methodological factors, the differences between the $d$-values were in the same direction but were smaller and no longer reached significance, for fixed-effect adjusted $d$-values, $Q(1, k = 99) = 0.26$, *ns*, for random-effect adjusted $d$-values, $Q(1, k = 99) = 0.26$, *ns*.

*Class size and individualized instruction.* The number of students in each summer school class was associated with the magnitude of the $d$-indexes

## TABLE 8

### PROGRAM FEATURE MODERATORS OF REMEDIAL SUMMER SCHOOL EVALUATION OUTCOMES

| | | Unadjusted d-indexes | | | | | | Adjusted d-indexes | | | | | |
| | | Fixed | | | Random | | | Fixed | | | Random | | |
| Moderator | k | Q | d | +/-ci | Q | d | +/-ci | Q | d | +/-ci | Q | d | +/-ci |
|---|---|---|---|---|---|---|---|---|---|---|---|---|---|
| Volunteered | 99 | 50.06* | | | 5.14* | | | 0.26 | | | 0.26 | | |
| no[1] | 80 | | .29 | .02 | | .30 | .06 | | .27 | .02 | | .28 | .05 |
| yes | 19 | | .09 | .05 | | .10 | .09 | | .25 | .05 | | .21 | .11 |
| Class Size | 28 | 6.47* | | | 0.34 | | | 9.50* | | | 0.91 | | |
| <20 | 13 | | .38 | .06 | | .53 | .20 | | .39 | .06 | | .47 | .18 |
| >20 | 15 | | .24 | .05 | | .27 | .12 | | .19 | .05 | | .19 | .10 |
| Individual Instruction? | 99 | 165.20* | | | 18.16* | | | 61.41* | | | 10.32* | | |
| no[1] | 73 | | .15 | .03 | | .17 | .05 | | .20 | .03 | | .21 | .05 |
| yes | 26 | | .43 | .03 | | .47 | .07 | | .37 | .03 | | .42 | .10 |
| Residential? | 99 | 12.60* | | | 0.79 | | | 4.38* | | | 0.18 | | |
| no[1] | 91 | | .25 | .02 | | .25 | .06 | | .26 | .02 | | .26 | .05 |
| yes | 8 | | .41 | .09 | | .40 | .14 | | .36 | .09 | | .33 | .13 |
| Parent Involvement? | 99 | 9.96* | | | 13.06* | | | 9.08* | | | 11.33* | | |
| no[1] | 91 | | .25 | .02 | | .24 | .05 | | .26 | .02 | | .24 | .05 |
| yes | 8 | | .54 | .18 | | .90 | .61 | | .53 | .17 | | .78 | .53 |
| Amount of Instruction | 67 | 7.12* | | | 2.02 | | | 0.00 | | | 0.00 | | |
| <60 hrs | 17 | | .20 | .06 | | .27 | .14 | | .34 | .06 | | .28 | .11 |
| 60 to 120 hrs | 34 | | .37 | .04 | | .38 | .10 | | .28 | .04 | | .33 | .11 |
| >120 hrs | 16 | | .21 | .05 | | .20 | .11 | | .29 | .05 | | .34 | .09 |
| Curriculum Content | 52 | 10.30* | | | 5.97 | | | 25.72* | | | 3.12 | | |
| reading | 9 | | .22 | .07 | | .41 | .23 | | .43 | .07 | | .43 | .11 |
| math and reading | 16 | | .40 | .04 | | .37 | .09 | | .30 | .04 | | .25 | .13 |
| multiple subjects | 27 | | .20 | .04 | | .19 | .06 | | .22 | .04 | | .24 | .06 |

[1]Includes samples from reports that did not mention this moderator.

*p < .05.

## TABLE 9
### Measurement Moderators of Summer School Evaluation Outcomes

| Moderator | k | Unadjusted d-indexes | | | | | | Adjusted d-indexes | | | | | |
|---|---|---|---|---|---|---|---|---|---|---|---|---|---|
| | | Fixed | | | Random | | | Fixed | | | Random | | |
| | | Q | d | +/-ci | Q | d | +/-ci | Q | d | +/-ci | Q | d | +/-ci |
| Measurement Delay | 81 | 33.64* | | | 10.40* | | | 4.83* | | | 1.57 | | |
| none | 35 | | .32 | .03 | | .31 | .07 | | .31 | .03 | | .29 | .07 |
| Sept. or Oct. | 30 | | .17 | .06 | | .17 | .08 | | .24 | .06 | | .24 | .06 |
| later | 16 | | .06 | .12 | | .06 | .12 | | .25 | .12 | | .24 | .14 |
| Outcome Metric | 87 | 3.43 | | | 0.90 | | | 0.10 | | | 0.10 | | |
| raw scores | 72 | | .28 | .03 | | .28 | .07 | | .26 | .03 | | .28 | .06 |
| norm-referred | 15 | | .24 | .04 | | .21 | .09 | | .27 | .04 | | .21 | .09 |
| Outcome Content | 165 | 27.60* | | | 1.03 | | | 6.34 | | | 0.68 | | |
| reading | 87 | | .22 | .02 | | .25 | .06 | | .24 | .02 | | .26 | .06 |
| math | 64 | | .30 | .03 | | .27 | .06 | | .27 | .03 | | .26 | .06 |
| general academic | 4 | | .08 | .17 | | .19 | .33 | | .33 | .17 | | .33 | .17 |
| nonacademic | 10 | | .18 | .09 | | .16 | .13 | | .18 | .09 | | .19 | .18 |

*$p < .05$.

under fixed-effect assumptions, for unadjusted $d$-values, $Q(1,k = 28) = 6.47$, $p < .02$, for adjusted $d$-values, $Q(1,k = 28) = 9.50$, $p < .005$, but not under random-effect assumptions, for unadjusted $d$-values, $Q(1,k = 28) = 0.34$, $ns$, for adjusted $d$-values, $Q(1,k = 28) = 0.91$, $ns$. To illustrate, programs with fewer than 20 students in a class revealed $d$-values ranging from .38 to .53, whereas programs with more than 20 students per class revealed $d$-values ranging from .19 to .27.

Whether or not the program was described as involving individualized instruction revealed a robust relationship to outcomes. All four analyses showed that programs using individualized instruction had larger effects associated with them, $d$-values ranged from .37 to .47, than programs that did not or did not mention how students were grouped, $d$-values ranged from .15 to .21, for fixed-effect unadjusted $d$-values, $Q(1,k = 99) = 165.20$, $p < .0001$, for random-effect unadjusted $d$-values, $Q(1,k = 99) = 18.16$, $p < .0001$, for fixed-effect adjusted $d$-values, $Q(1,k = 99) = 61.41$, $p < .0001$, for random-effect adjusted $d$-values, $Q(1,k = 99) = 10.32$, $p < .005$.

Our examination of outliers highlighted a program that employed individualized instruction (Cramer & Dorsey, 1969). We found 12 other evaluations that stated instruction was given to students individually. Four of these programs involved students with learning or other disabilities (Franklin, 1987; Leviton, 1973; Menousek, 1983; Miller et al., 1987), and three others have been described because of other design features (Cobb et al., 1990; Curry, 1990; Siegelman, 1975). The remaining five programs also deserve brief descriptions.

Amorose (1987) reported on a summer program conducted for the Columbus, Ohio, public schools that focused on reading and math skills of at-risk high school students. Interestingly, participants were paid to attend classes. The program met for 39 days and both homogeneous and heterogeneous class groupings were used along with individualized instruction. Pretest-posttest scores revealed a $d$-value of .50. Tam (1987) also evaluated a program in Columbus, Ohio, that ran during 1987. This program was for 2nd graders who were experiencing difficulties in reading. The 24-day program involved 30 min of one-on-one reading instruction each day. The resulting $d$-value was .74.

Brown (1991) evaluated a residential camping program in South Carolina for predominantly African American boys and girls. Camp lasted for 3 to 4 weeks and mornings at camp were spent in academic activities. Pretest-to-posttest effects ranged from $d = .31$ to .48.

Merkel-Keller (1987) described a program for 10th graders in New Jersey. This program also included both academic instruction and paid employment. Three hours of instruction lasted for 6 weeks and was provided in groups of students as small as five, with intensive teacher input, involvement, and interaction. The resulting $d$-value was .16.

Finally, Woloshin (1975) examined a New York City summer program meant to overcome reading and math deficiencies in 9th and 10th graders. Three hours of instruction occurred for 6 weeks. Individualized instruction was preceded by the use of standardized tests to diagnose each student's strengths and weaknesses and instruction was based on these results. Effect sizes were $d = .42$ and $.47$. In sum then, both the class size and individualized instruction findings strongly suggest that greater opportunities for attention to individual students is associated with larger positive effects of summer school.

*Residential programs.* Five evaluations containing eight independent samples described programs that involved students taking up residence away from home during the summer program. The evaluations by Brown (1991), just described because of its use of individualized instruction, and by Curry (1990), described because it used random assignment, revealed positive summer school effects ranging from $d = .29$ to $.48$.

A summer program with the goal of preventing rural, economically disadvantaged youths from dropping out of school was evaluated by Wells, Springer, and McCready (1987). The program included academic, vocational, and counseling components. Students remained in residence halls at Louisiana Tech University. Counseling was provided by both full-time counselors and by specially trained undergraduate university students. Questionnaires sent to the students' high school principals revealed that all participants were enrolled in school the following year. Large gains were made from pretest to posttest achievement measures, averaging $d = .77$ for the sample.

Improved academics and academic motivation in adolescent boys who were at-risk and who had demonstrated behavior problems was the focus of a brief residential summer program evaluated by Rawson (1992, 1993). The program was assessed over two summers with different measures given each summer. Small groups of students were taught by a teacher and a "therapist" whose job it was to keep children on task. The different subject matters were taught in summer camp–type settings rather than in classrooms. For example, reading instruction occurred at camp crafts and science in nature study. In 1992, the dependent measure was students' intrinsic motivation for academic study. Comparisons of preprogram and postprogram scores revealed $d$-values ranging from $.19$ to $.31$, with improvements in intrinsic motivation for all subject areas, especially reading.

The results of the meta-analysis revealed that these residential programs were associated with larger effect sizes, with $d$-values ranging from $.33$ to $.41$, than nonresidential programs, with $d$-values ranging from $.25$ to $.26$, under fixed-effect assumptions but not random-effect assumptions, for fixed-effect unadjusted $d$-values, $Q(1, k = 99) = 12.60$, $p < .0005$, for random-effect unadjusted $d$-values, $Q(1, k = 99) = 0.79$, *ns*, for fixed-effect adjusted $d$-values, $Q(1, k = 99) = 4.38$, $p < .04$, for random effect adjusted $d$-values, $Q(1, k = 99) = 0.18$, *ns*.

*Parent involvement.* Reports explicitly stating that the program they described had some requirement that parents be involved in the summer school revealed larger effects, with $d$-values ranging from .53 to .90, than programs without such a requirement or that did not state such a requirement existed, with $d$-values ranging from .24 to .26. This finding was robust across both types of statistical models and both unadjusted and adjusted $d$-indexes, for fixed-effect unadjusted $d$-values, $Q(1, k = 99) = 9.96$, $p < .005$, for random-effect unadjusted $d$-values, $Q(1, k = 99) = 13.06$, $p < .0005$, for fixed-effect adjusted $d$-values, $Q(1, k = 99) = 9.08$, $p < .005$, for random-effect adjusted $d$-values, $Q(1, k = 99) = 11.33$, $p < .001$. When we examined the three reports that contributed independent samples to this analysis, however, we found that five samples came from the study by Cramer and Dorsey (1969) that provided effect sizes that were Winsorized to a value of $d = 1.50$. Two effect sizes came from Culp (1973), one of the few studies that produced uniformly negative effects. The eighth sample came from Geis (1968), mentioned earlier because it employed random assignment. This $d$-value was .15. Thus, although the programs with parent involvement components produce large average effects that are reliably different from other programs, the evidence we have on these programs is minimal and shows great variation in effect estimates.

*Amount of instruction.* The homogeneity analysis examining the relationship between the number of hours of instruction in the summer program and the program's effect proved significant only when unadjusted $d$-values were tested using fixed-effect assumptions, for fixed-effect unadjusted $d$-values, $Q(1, k = 67) = 7.12$, $p < .01$, for random-effect unadjusted $d$-values, $Q(1, k = 67) = 2.02$, *ns*, for fixed-effect adjusted $d$-values, $Q(1, k = 67) = 0.00$, *ns*, for random-effect adjusted $d$-values, $Q(1, k = 67) = 0.00$, *ns*. An examination of a three-way breakout of fixed-effect, unadjusted $d$-values, however, suggested a curvilinear component, with summer programs lasting less than 60 hr showing an effects of $d = .20$, programs lasting between 60 and 120 hr a $d = .37$, or more than 120 hr a $d = .21$.

*Curriculum content.* The content of the summer curriculum was significantly or near-significantly related to the summer program outcomes in three of the four analyses, for fixed-effect unadjusted $d$-values, $Q(2, k = 52) = 10.30$, $p < .01$, for random-effect unadjusted $d$-values, $Q(2, k = 52) = 5.97$, $p < .06$, for fixed-effect adjusted $d$-values, $Q(2, k = 52) = 25.72$, $p < .0001$, for random-effect adjusted $d$-values, $Q(2, k = 52) = 3.12$, *ns*. The pattern of relationships between effect sizes for programs primarily focusing on reading curricula, on both reading and math curricula, and on multiple subjects, however, does not remain stable across model assumptions and statistical adjustments. Whereas d-values for programs with multiple-subject curricula tend to remain stable, ranging from .19 to .24, the reading and math program outcomes vary in magnitude from $d = .25$ to .40, and reading-only programs vary most of all, from $d = .22$ to .43.

An examination of the six studies that contributed the nine samples in the reading curriculum category revealed that seven of the samples had d-values that ranged from .06 to .48, but the remaining two samples provided exceptionally large d-values (from Baxley & Hinton, 1971, $d = 1.45$ and from Welch & Jensen, 1990, $d = 1.50$). Thus, the highly variable average estimates are likely a function of the shifting weight given these two studies in the calculation of each estimate.

## TESTS FOR MEASUREMENT MODERATORS OF EVALUATION OUTCOMES

Three measurement characteristics were tested as moderators of the effects of summer school. The results of these analyses are displayed in Table 9.

*Measurement delay.* A relatively robust association appeared, suggesting that longer delays in measuring a program's effect were associated with smaller d-values, especially under fixed-effect assumptions, for fixed-effect unadjusted d-values, $Q(1, k = 81) = 33.64$, $p < .0001$, for random-effect unadjusted d-values, $Q(1, k = 81) = 10.40$, $p < .005$, for fixed-effect adjusted d-values, $Q(1, k = 81) = 4.83$, $p < .03$, for random-effect adjusted d-values, $Q(1, k = 81) = 1.57$, *ns.*

When we examined the five studies that measured the effects of summer school with long delays, we found two evaluations, David (1974) and Leviton (1973), included multiple follow-up measures. David (1974) found a sharp decrease in effect sizes from a testing immediately following the summer program, $d = .58$, to the delayed measurement, $d = .18$, whereas Leviton (1973) found an increase from a September–October testing, $d = .27$, to a longer delay, $d = .44$.

Ward (1989) assessed the long-term effectiveness of North Carolina's Basic Education Summer School Program. The program was instituted as a remediation effort for academically at-risk 3rd and 6th graders. All eligible students from around the state were invited to participate and program participants were matched with nonparticipants of similar school, sex, ethnicity, and preprogram achievement test score. In addition to reading and math, participants were tested for the program's effects on general cognitive abilities and strategic processing of information. Results indicated that

75

the summer program effect was not sustained over 2 years. The researcher cautioned, however, that missing data, grade retention, and varied summer experiences over the 2-year follow-up complicated the evaluation. The follow-up measures produced one positive effect, $d = .03$, and one negative effect, $d = -.16$.

Menousek (1983) and Abram and Maurelli (1980), mentioned above, also had measures delayed beyond the fall of the following school year. Menousek (1983) found a negative effect of summer school, $d = -.13$. Abram and Maurelli (1980) examined the effects of a summer program in Owensboro, Kentucky. Very few differences were found when delayed measures were compared for summer school participants and nonparticipants, but the overall effect was positive, $d = .12$.

*Outcome metric.* None of the four analyses produced a significant relationship between the magnitude of the $d$-indexes and whether the outcome of the summer program was measured in raw scores or norm-referenced scores, for fixed-effect unadjusted $d$-values, $Q(1, k = 87) = 3.43$, $p < .07$, for random-effect unadjusted $d$-values, $Q(1, k = 87) = 0.90$, *ns*, for fixed-effect adjusted $d$-values, $Q(1, k = 87) = 0.10$, *ns*, for random-effect adjusted $d$-values, $Q(1, k = 87) = 0.10$, *ns*.

*Outcome content.* The subject matter content of the outcome measure proved to be a significant predictor of the effect size estimates only when we examined unadjusted $d$-values using fixed-effect assumptions, for fixed-effect unadjusted $d$-values, $Q(3, k = 165) = 27.60$, $p < .0001$, for random-effect unadjusted $d$-values, $Q(3, k = 165) = 1.03$, *ns*, for fixed-effect adjusted $d$-values, $Q(3, k = 165) = 6.34$, $p < .10$, for random-effect adjusted $d$-values, $Q(3, k = 165) = 0.68$, *ns*. Math-related measures, $d = .30$, revealed the largest effect of summer school, and measures of general academic achievement, $d = .08$, revealed the smallest effect, with reading measures, $d = .22$, and nonacademic measures, $d = .18$, falling in between. As with the curriculum content results, however, the pattern of relationships did not remain stable across the four analyses.

We also looked more closely at the evaluations that measured outcomes other than reading or math. Wasik and Sibley (1969), described earlier, examined a summer program for culturally disadvantaged students entering 1st grade. Preprogram to postprogram changes in standardized intelligence test scores showed dramatic effects, with two samples revealing $d$-indexes of .68 and .93. Ward (1989), also describe in detail above, found mixed effects on cognitive ability scores, $d = -.10$ and .06.

Six evaluations included nonacademic measures of summer school outcomes. "Beat the Odds" was an instructional, counseling, and guidance summer program sponsored by the Houston, Texas, schools to assist at-risk

5th through 9th graders. The program focused on both academic and sociopsychological deficiencies (Opuni et al., 1990). The program staff included teachers, educational diagnosticians, psychologists, social workers, and student tutors. Instruction occurred both individually and in groups, and counseling sessions were held as well. Teachers reported positive benefits from the in-service components that helped them instruct at-risk students. Participants described the major strengths of the program as its caring atmosphere and its small group instruction (although the actual size of the classes was not given). Weaknesses included a lack of time for informal meetings among staff, unnecessary instructional interruptions, and the short duration of the program (4 weeks). Student assessments of the program revealed an average positive effect on attitudes toward school and teachers, and self-esteem. No academic outcome measures were reported.

Leviton (1973), described above, included measures of student self-esteem and found mixed results, with effects ranging from $d = -.04$ to $d = .32$. Ward (1989), just mentioned for inclusion of general cognitive measures, included a measure of student absences during the following school year. The postprogram comparisons generally showed participants had more absences than nonparticipants. Brown (1991), Curry (1990), and Rawson (1992) also contributed effect sizes to the calculation of effects on nonacademic outcomes.

*A demonstration of meta-analysis using comparisons generated within studies.* The outcome content data set provided us with an opportunity to demonstrate a very powerful meta-analytic technique. Recall that for some moderator variables a single evaluation could contribute more than one effect size if it collected data on more than one moderator category. For example, in our examination of sex differences in summer school outcomes, we were able to identify a few studies that included both males and females and gave separate results for each sex. Similarly, two evaluations were found that tested summer school outcomes with different lengths of delay. These evaluations can be highly informative, because they control internally for many of the methodological confounds (known and unknown) that weaken the inferences achievable through meta-analysis. That is, when an evaluation breaks out the effect of the program for males and females separately, we can be relatively confident that many other aspects of the program did not covary with the student's sex. The length of the program, instructional practices, and testing conditions ought to be about the same for both males and females.

This within-study control is even stronger when we consider evaluations that include both a measure of reading and a measure of math achievement. Here, not only are all program-related variations controlled by the within-study multiple measurements (unless different programs focused on

77

one skill area but measured both reading and math, which is rarely if ever the case), but student variations are controlled as well, because each student takes both subject area tests. Therefore, as a final means for examining the outcome content findings, we identified each of the evaluations that included both a reading and a math outcome measured on the same students. By looking at these studies separately, we could determine whether the outcome content difference emerged within evaluations in which other components of the program were held constant. There were 21 evaluations, including 56 independent samples that used both reading and math outcome measures. All but three of these evaluations have been described already.

A summer program conducted in Milwaukee, Wisconsin (Gousha, 1968), prevailed on teachers to rely heavily on the use of city and neighborhood resources for field trips. Positive effects were found on both math, $d = .29$, and reading skills, $d = .22$. Teachers reported a lack of time for instruction and delays or waiting for supplies were the greatest weaknesses of the program.

An Austin, Texas, summer program for 7th and 8th grade retainees was evaluated during the summer of 1980 (Porterfield & Eglasaer, 1980). The program's objectives were to improve basic academic skills and decision-making skills. Results revealed that 7th graders made significant gains on math computation skills, whereas 8th graders showed significant gains on three subtests of the Iowa Test of Basic Skills. Overall, the math $d$-value was $d = .79$ and reading $d$-value was $d = .21$. The decision-making curriculum was reported not to have met its objectives, although no data on these outcomes were provided.

Improvement in reading and math achievement of at-risk and failing 4th through 8th grade students was the objective of a summer program examined by Hyman (1988). Preprogram versus postprogram testing revealed general improvement in both achievement and attitudes towards the two subjects, with somewhat greater effects on reading achievement, $d = .40$, than math achievement, $d = .24$.

Overall, 13 of the 21 evaluations produced evidence that the summer program had larger effects on math than on reading. In 32 of the 56 independent samples, the effect on math was larger than the accompanying effect on reading. In these samples, the weighted average effect of summer school on reading outcomes was $d = .22$, and on math $d = .28$.

The fact that these 56 samples had measures of both reading and math increases our ability to make strong inferences about causal differences, because we know many other methodological and substantive variations are equally represented in the reading and math "conditions." It also permits us to increase the power of our statistical tests by removing from our estimate of error variation in math and reading effects due to differences in summer programs. Such an analysis proceeds as follows. First, in order to determine whether the difference between the average program effect on reading and math was reliable, we calculated the difference between the reading and math $d$-values within each independent sample. These can be viewed as effect sizes in their own right. Then, using both fixed-effect and random-effect assumptions, we calculated the weighted average of the differences in $d$-values and their confidence intervals. So, for the fixed-effect model, the average $d$-value difference was .065 with a 95% confidence interval from $d = .035$ to .10. For the random-effect model, the average $d$-value difference was .04 with a 95% confidence interval from $d = -.06$ to .14. Thus, under fixed-effect assumptions, we can reject the null hypothesis that the effect of summer school was equal for math and reading, with the average difference suggesting more favorable outcomes on math tests. Under random-effect assumptions, the null hypothesis could not be rejected.

## MISCELLANEOUS STUDIES

There are only two evaluations that have not received mention thus far. First, a summer program carried out in New York City in 1967 (Fox & Weinberg, 1967) involved 470 junior high students taking remedial instruction in reading and math. This program contained the unique feature of using recent high school graduates from disadvantaged neighborhoods to assist classroom teachers as educational aides. The study also included numerous process questionnaires distributed to teachers, aides, supervisors, and students. Generally, teachers felt students benefited from the program, but nearly all teachers believed that some students did not. Across most groups, the major weakness of the program was described as a lack of planning time before instruction began. Concerns aside, the evaluation revealed the program had positive effects on reading scores, $d = .17$, and even larger effects on math scores, $d = .37$.

Second, an evaluation by D'Agostino and Hiestand (1995) examined a summer program for disadvantaged 4th graders in Chicago, Illinois. This study was unique because it included an observation and categorization of summer school classrooms based on how much focus was placed on advanced or authentic instruction. These types of instruction were defined as including encouragement of student problem-solving, and critical and creative thinking, among other instructional strategies. This evaluation also employed Rasch measurement procedures and hierarchical linear modeling of the program's effect. The evaluators reported that classrooms with a greater focus on advanced learning skills contained students who made greater yearly math and reading gains. Regardless of the instructional distinction, the studies also revealed that summer school students made positive pretest-to-posttest gains in reading and math, but did more poorly than a matched control group.

# VI. NARRATIVE AND META-ANALYTIC SYNTHESIS OF PROGRAMS FOR ACCELERATION OF LEARNING

Seven other evaluations, including 34 independent samples and 60 comparisons, assessed the effects of summer programs that were meant to accelerate learning. Table 10 summarizes important characteristics of these studies.

## NARRATIVE DESCRIPTION OF ACCELERATION PROGRAM EVALUATIONS

Winston (1963) evaluated a 6-week summer program for 4th or 5th grade gifted children. Class sizes were about 13 and teachers served more as resource consultants than active instructors. The program took place in the local high school. Within a generally flexible structure, the program focused on the content areas of science and language arts. Approximately 50 participants were matched with 50 nonparticipants based on age, sex, grade, IQ, achievement, and socioeconomic status. Results suggested no significant effects of the summer program on science and most nonacademic measures. The $d$-values for four independent samples, however, ranged from $d = .31$ to $d = .60$.

Hayes and Kerr (1970) evaluated a summer program conducted in rural Virginia. This program identified students who were economically disadvantaged but had demonstrated academic talents. The program had both academic and cultural objectives, hoping to broaden children's range of cultural experiences. Results on formal testing were mixed, with the three $d$-values for independent samples at $d = -.33$, $d = -.03$, and $d = .40$, and no clear pattern of improvement in either academics or self-esteem. A questionnaire completed by both students and observers pointed to an unstructured atmosphere and lost instructional time due to logistical problems as the program's most important shortcomings.

Brody (1984) examined the effects of an intensive summer program on the SAT scores of gifted students identified through the Johns Hopkins

## TABLE 10

### MEAN EFFECT SIZE BY INDEPENDENT SAMPLE FOR ACCELERATION AS THE GOAL

| First Author | Year of Report (Program) | Location | Number of Students in Analyses | Grade | Achievement Label | Type of Comparison | Outcome Measure | $d$ = Index Range ($n$) |
|---|---|---|---|---|---|---|---|---|
| Winston | 1963 | Plainview, NY | 102 | 4th & 5th | Gifted | Post-post | Language, needs, science | .31 to .60(4) |
| Hayes | 1970 (1968) | Nelson County, VA | 100 | 9th–11th | Gifted | Post-post and pre-post | Self-esteem; Science & self-esteem; World culture & self-esteem | -.32 to .40(3) |
| Brody | 1984 (1983) | Baltimore, MD | 776 | 7th | Gifted | Post-post | Math & verbal | -.74 to 1.82(16) |
| Klein | 1970 (1966) | New Haven, CT | 72 | 10th | Average | Post-post | Math, SAT, & class standing | .00(1) |
| Kulieke | 1986 (1984) | Chicago, IL | 125 | 6th–9th | Gifted | Pre-post | Attitudes about achievement & science | .18 to .74(3) |
| Olszewski | 1987 | Chicago, IL | 456 | 7th–11th | Gifted | Pre-post | Attitudes about achievement | -.10 to .04(4) |
| Kolloff | 1989 (1985) | Northern CO & West Lafayette, IN | 508 | 5th–11th | Gifted | Pre-post | Self-esteem | .22 to .37(3) |

*Note.* The number of students in analyses is the sum of sample sizes for each independent sample; as such, it includes *n*s for both pre-post and post-post analyses.

Talent Search. Students who were eligible for the program but chose not to attend served as controls. Sixteen independent samples contributed $d$-indexes ranging in value from $d = -.74$ to the two largest values in this set of studies, $d = 1.82$ and $d = 1.69$. Overall, the program had no effect on scores on the verbal portion of the SAT but was associated with higher math scores. No interaction effects involving the sex of the student were found.

Klein and Gould (1970) evaluated the Yale Summer High School program. This program involved 100 students entering the 11th grade who were nominated by their schools because they had high intellectual capacity, were underachieving, and came from economically disadvantaged homes. More students were nominated than could attend the program and participants were chosen randomly from those nominated. Multiple follow-up assessments were taken, up to 2 years after the end of the program. Results were mixed but generally revealed little difference between students who attended the program and students who did not, with an average $d$-value for the sample of $d = .00$. The author speculated that because students in both the summer school and control groups were gifted, eventually they would all be recognized and rewarded by their local high school. Put differently, Klein and Gould speculated that control group students eventually received benefits similar to those received by students attending the Yale program.

Kulieke (1986) and Olszewski, Kulieke, and Willis (1987) evaluated two separate years of three acceleration programs conducted in the Chicago, Illinois, area. Aimed at gifted middle school students, the programs focused on science and math instruction. They also gave students the opportunity to interact with practicing scientists and to acquire skills associated with application of the scientific method. One program was run at the Argonne National Laboratory, and two at Northwestern University. For the first evaluation, preprogram to postprogram changes in attitudes toward science, self-esteem, and the College Board Achievement Test in Biology served as the outcome measures. The effects on achievement scores were very positive, but mixed results were found on the non-academic measures. Similar mixed findings were found during the second evaluation on a measure of global self-worth.

Kolloff and Moore (1989) presented data on the self-concepts of 508 gifted 5th through 10th grade students who took part in three residential summer programs. One program ran at the University of Northern Colorado and two ran at Purdue University. In all three programs, students chose courses from numerous alternatives taught by college faculty. Two measures of self concept revealed $d$-values of preprogram to postprogram change ranging from .22 to .37. No differences in the effect of the programs were found based on the sex or grade level of the student.

## META-ANALYSIS OF ACCELERATION PROGRAM EVALUATIONS

As with the meta-analysis of remedial programs, first we Winsorized extreme $d$-values so that no comparison contributed an effect size larger than $d = 1.50$ (necessary in four cases). No sample size was larger than 500 or condition size larger than 250. A total of approximately 2,200 students took part in the evaluations.

Of the 60 comparisons, 18 produced negative values. Of 34 independent samples, 9 produced average negative effects across all outcome measures (see Figure 1). The average unweighted $d$-value across the 34 independent samples was $d = .23$. The median effect size was $d = .25$. When the contribution of samples was weighted by their sample sizes the average $d$-value under fixed-effect assumptions was $d = .16$. The 95% confidence interval for the weighted $d$-value ranged from .10 to .21. Under random-effect assumptions, the weighted average $d$-index was .18, with a 95% confidence interval ranging from .07 to 30. Thus, we can reject the null hypothesis that summer programs with the goal of accelerating student achievement had no effect. Students in these programs outperformed their own pretest scores or the posttest comparison group by about one sixth of a standard deviation.

The fixed-effect homogeneity analysis revealed much greater variation in $d$-values than would be expected from sampling error alone, $Q(1, k = 34) = 98.56$, $p < .0001$. Our examination of the codes for moderator variables, however, revealed too much missing data and/or widely disparate numbers of independent samples within code categories for us to place great faith in the outcomes of any formal tests of the moderating effects of methodological, student, program, or outcome characteristics. Because they were of high interest, we did run analyses looking at effect size differences between students below and above grade 8, between residential and non-residential programs, and between different contents for the outcome measure. In no case did we find these to be significant moderators of summer school effects.

# VII. NARRATIVE AND META-ANALYTIC SYNTHESIS OF PROGRAMS WITH OTHER AND MULTIPLE GOALS

Seven evaluations, including 20 independent samples and 32 comparisons, examined summer programs that had goals other than remediation or acceleration or had multiple goals that were not tested independently. Approximately 3,100 students were included in these samples. Table 11 provides some pertinent information on each study.

## NARRATIVE DESCRIPTION OF OTHER AND MULTIPLE GOAL PROGRAM EVALUATIONS

The earliest report of such a program we were able to obtain was an assessment of a 1965 Human Development Project carried out in Richmond, Virginia, schools and cosponsored by the Ford Foundation (Tyler, 1966). The program included a variety of activities in the area of language arts, reading, speech, and arts and crafts that were either remedial or enrichment in focus. This evaluation included teacher responses to questionnaires, as well as preprogram and postprogram comparisons of achievement test scores, and delayed achievement test comparisons between students at schools who did and did not have the summer program. Generally, teachers rated remedial activities as having the greatest value. Preprogram versus postprogram analyses of achievement data revealed significant positive effects on reading and language skills and nonsignificant positive effects on arithmetic. This was not surprising, given that math-related activities were not a large component of the summer program. The effect sizes for the two independent samples included in this evaluation were $d = .46$ and $d = .51$. Teachers reported they felt students' academic skills improved somewhat more than expected but felt more positive gains occurred in student attitudes than achievement. No differences in preprogram versus postprogram scores were found based on the sex of the student, but students

## TABLE 11

### Mean Effect Size by Independent Sample for Multiple Goals

| First Author | Year of Report (Program) | Location | Number of Students in Analyses | Grade | Achievement Label | Type of Comparison | Outcome Measure | d-Index Range (n) |
|---|---|---|---|---|---|---|---|---|
| Tyler | 1966 (1965) | Rural VA | 307 | 4th–6th | ? | Pre-post | Language, math, & reading | .23 to .26 (2) |
| Heyns | 1978 | Atlanta, GA | 1504 | 6th | Average | Post-post | Reading | .14 (2) |
| Klibanoff | 1981 | National | 2009 | 2nd & 6th | Varied | Pre-post | Math & reading | .06 to .24 (5) |
| Ashton | 1983 | Detroit, MI | 451 | k–12th | Academically disadvantaged | Pre-post | Reading | .12 to .64 (4) |
| Karnes | 1987 (1985) | Two small cities | 110 | 7th–12th | Average | Pre-post | Leadership | 1.51 to 2.95 (2) |
| Oliphant | 1988 | San Rafael, CA | 443 | 1st–2nd | Varied | Post-post and pre-post | Math & reading | .57 (1) |
| Thompson | 1989 (1988) | Chicago, IL | 46 | 7th–8th | Average | Pre-post | Self-esteem | –.57 to 2.89 (4) |

*Note.* The number of students in analyses is the sum of sample sizes for each independent sample; as such, it includes *n*s for both pre-post and post-post analyses.

with IQ scores above 85 were found to benefit more than students with IQ scores below 85. Comparisons between schools that did and did not take part in the project were difficult to interpret, because scores were compared for the schools as a whole and it is not clear from the report how comparison schools were chosen.

Heyns (1978) provided what is perhaps the most thorough and informative evaluation of summer school. She examined the impact on 6th graders of a large, voluntary, free-tuition, summer program conducted in 23 different Atlanta, Georgia, public schools in 1972. The program was disproportionately likely to be used by Black families, even when the SES of families was controlled. A wide variety of courses was offered on diverse topics, including everything from arts and sports to remedial classes. On average, however, participants' achievement levels were equal or above those of nonattendees, and only a small fraction of students were enrolled in order to make up academic work. Attendance varied greatly from school to school, ranging from 55% to 89%. Heyns examined questionnaires completed by students, teachers, principals, and parents along with student scores on a word recognition test, said to be indicative of scores on other tests as well. All parties agreed the program was a success. Teachers invariably mentioned small class sizes, allowing informal and individualized instruction, and greater personal autonomy as the causes of success. Children reported that summer school was fun. Parents praised the program for keeping children off the streets. This was especially true of comments by working mothers, who were also disproportionately likely to have children in the program. Heyns broke out the achievement data by comparing grade-level equivalent gain scores of program participants and nonparticipants according to the length of the program, the school attended, and the race and economic background of the child. Children who were enrolled for more than 6 weeks consistently gained more than those attending less than 6 weeks. Children who attended a summer program given in a building other then the one they regularly attended showed the largest gains. White students appeared to gain about 2.5 months on the test whether or not they attended summer school, $d = -.01$. Black students who did not attend lost about 1.8 months compared to 0.3 months for Black students who attended summer school, $d = .14$. Finally, a substantial interaction appeared involving the economic background of the student. Students from the most advantaged families consistently showed the most gain from summer school. Heyns concluded that summer sessions, unlike regular sessions, "tend to amplify rather than diminish cognitive inequities" (p. 136).

The evaluation by Klibanoff and Haggart (1981) that looked at remedial programs also included five nonremedial samples. These sample $d$-indexes varied in value from $d = .05$ to $d = .23$.

A columnist for the *Detroit News* founded the "Let's Read" summer program. Ashton (1983) conducted an evaluation of the program. The program used a specific reading curriculum that emphasized letter and word recognition skills. Nonprofessional volunteers were used as reading instructors and parents of students under age 13 were required to be involved through attendance at some summer sessions. Participation was voluntary, parents registered their child on given days, but materials had to be purchased by the family. Results revealed that program participants showed improvement in reading scores from preprogram to postprogram and that gain was related to the number of lessons completed by the student. The $d$-values for four independent samples ranged from $d = .12$ to $d = .64$.

Karnes, Meriweather, and D'Llio (1987) described and evaluated a program meant to develop the leadership skills of average to gifted students in 6th through 11th grade. Students identified their own areas of need through the use of a leadership skills inventory that assessed nine different skills, including writing, speech, values clarification, group dynamics, and planning. Teachers then assisted students in choosing appropriate activities. Preprogram to postprogram comparisons of scores on the inventory revealed extremely large effects for both the 1st year, $d = 1.51$, and 2nd year, $d = 2.95$, of the program.

Oliphant (1988) evaluated a summer program conducted in San Rafael, California, 2 years after it took place. A nonequivalent group comparison was made by using as controls all students in the school district who did not attend summer school. The overall $d$-value for the evaluation was $d = .53$, including one comparison with a $d$-value of 1.66 that was Winsorized to $d = 1.50$. The data were also analyzed, however, broken out by English-proficient and nonproficient students. Results revealed that English-proficient students who attended summer school made significantly greater academic gains when compared to similar students who did not attend summer classes. Summer school had no effect on students who were not proficient in English. In general, the author questions the value of summer school.

Finally, Thompson (1989) reported on a Chicago, Illinois, summer program for disadvantaged girls that was undertaken with multiple goals in mind. The program started out as a tutoring, sports, and trade program but then expanded to goals of academic achievement and character development. The character development aspects of the program focused on improving self-image to provide a basis for resisting drug and gang involvement. Students took classes in math and science, communication skills, character development, fine arts, and team sports. The program served primarily African American and Hispanic students in 7th through 9th grades.

A single measure of self-esteem revealed $d$-values ranging from $d = -.57$ to 2.89.

## META-ANALYSIS OF ACCELERATION PROGRAM EVALUATIONS

The seven evaluations of summer programs with multiple goals contained 32 comparisons taken from 20 independent samples (see Figure 1). Five comparisons generated extremely large $d$-values and were adjusted to $d = 1.50$. Even after adjustment, however, the average unweighted $d$-value based on independent samples was .48, but the median was .25.

Examination of the 20 sample effects revealed that only 1 was negative and 15 fell between $d$-values of .06 and .65. The fixed-effect model average weighted $d$-value was .26, with a 95% confidence interval ranging from .22 to .30. The random-effects estimate was $d = .38$, ranging from .25 to .51. Thus, we can reject the null hypothesis that summer programs with goals other than remediation and acceleration or with multiple goals had no effect on participants. Students in these programs outperformed their own pretest scores or the posttest comparison group by about one quarter of a standard deviation.

The fixed-effect homogeneity analysis revealed much greater variation in $d$-values than would be expected from sampling error alone, $Q(1, k = 20) = 153.31$, $p < .0001$. More so than with the evaluations of programs for acceleration, moderator variables revealed too much missing data and/or widely disparate numbers of independent samples within code categories for formal tests of the moderating effects of methodological, student, program, or outcome characteristics.

# VIII. DISCUSSION

Our discussion is divided into five sections. First, we summarize the major findings of the review. Careful attention is paid to assessing the overall trustworthiness of findings and to placing findings in the context of aligned areas of research, especially summer learning loss. Second, we attempt to interpret the overall findings of the meta-analysis by placing the summer school effect into a broader context that compares it to other educational interventions. Third, we make recommendations concerning what we believe are the most important directions for future research. Fourth, we make recommendations concerning the types of research methodologies that should be used in future studies. Clearly, future research on summer school would benefit greatly from improvements in design, measurement, and reporting. Finally, we bring our efforts together by making some specific recommendations concerning how summer programs with educational goals ought to be funded, planned, implemented, and evaluated.

## A SUMMARY AND ASSESSMENT OF FACTORS ASSOCIATED WITH SUMMER PROGRAM EFFECTS

We think there are five principal conclusions that can be drawn from this research synthesis. Our confidence in these conclusions is considerable because of the magnitude of effect, the elimination of plausible rival hypotheses, the number and size of the samples that tested the relationship under consideration, and the robustness across both fixed-effect and random-effect models.

First, *summer school programs focused on lessening or removing learning deficiencies have a positive impact on the knowledge and skills of participants. Overall, students completing remedial summer programs can be expected to score about one fifth of a standard deviation, or between one seventh and one quarter of a standard deviation, higher than the control group on outcome measures.* We base this conclusion on the convergence of numerous estimates of summer school

89

effects. First, the rough vote-count estimates of effect size ranged from $d = .10$ to $d = .49$. Second, the median effect size was $d = .19$. Third, the weighted average $d$-value across all samples was $d = .26$. This value had a 95% confidence interval ranging from .24 to .28 under fixed-effect assumptions and from .21 to .31 under random-effect assumptions.

These findings would support a conclusion that the positive effect of summer school was about one quarter of a standard deviation. It could be argued, however, that this estimate is inflated by the inclusion of evaluations using a pretest-posttest design. Pretest-posttest estimates might benefit from history, maturation, and regression-to-the mean effects confounded with summer school effects. They also might be inflated by the use of grade-equivalent test scores that increase over time simply due to their metric. Countervailing this inflation, the pretest-posttest estimates of summer school effects might be diminished by their neglect of summer learning loss in nonparticipating students.

Offsetting this possible inflation of our overall estimate was the inclusion in the meta-analysis of evaluations that used postprogram control groups that were imperfectly matched with summer school attendees. Given that these summer programs focused on lessening or removing learning deficiencies, it is likely that the imperfect-matched control groups contained students who, on average, were performing better than summer program participants prior to the program's implementation. Therefore, the imperfect-matched control group studies likely contained a selection bias that mitigated the estimate of the summer program effect. One of the smallest average effects appeared in evaluations that compared nonequivalent groups with or without an attempt to ensure their similarity to summer school attendees ($d = .05$, fixed-effect model). Within these designs, evaluations with better controls generally showed larger effects of summer school. Specifically, evaluations that matched on achievement showed a more positive effect of summer school ($d = .11$, fixed-effect, $d = .14$, random-effect) than evaluations that matched on other variables ($d = -.03$, both fixed-effect and random-effect).

Given that both pretest-posttest and nonequivalent-group designs are open to bias, it is important to examine carefully the results of evaluations that employed random assignment of students to summer school and control conditions and then measured outcomes for the two groups simultaneously. The evaluations that used random assignment revealed an average effect size, $d = .14$ (both fixed-effect and random-effect), that was somewhat smaller than the overall average effect size, although it was still significantly different from $d = 0$ (under both fixed-effect and random-effect assumptions). Therefore, in our summary statement about the literature, we chose to set the lower expectation of the summer school effect at the estimate generated by evaluations using random assignment (one seventh of a standard deviation) and the upper expectation at the value generated by the weighted average of all evaluations (one quarter of a standard deviation). These values seem quite reasonable, and perhaps a bit conservative, in the context of the entire constellation of estimates we derived.

We also should be clear that the overall impact of summer school should be viewed as an average effect found across a diverse group of programs evaluated with a wide variety of methods. As our moderator analyses revealed, these variations influence the effect size estimate in significant ways, to be addressed below. Put in practical terms, the overall estimate of effect could guide policy decisions at the broadest level, say by federal or state policymakers. A local official about to implement a specific summer program for a particular type of student, however, may find effects quite different from the overall finding. This official might consult our tables to find estimates more specific to the student and program characteristics most descriptive of his or her local effort. Generally, however, both our overall confidence intervals and those associated with specific categories of programs suggest it is unlikely the positive effect of most programs will be zero.

Second, *summer school programs focusing on acceleration of learning or on other or multiple goals also have a positive impact on participants roughly equal to programs focusing on remediation.* Our analyses of these programs revealed positive effects significantly different from $d = 0$ using either fixed-effect or random-effect model assumptions. Because of the smaller number of evaluations, however, we were reluctant to test for the robustness of these findings across methodological, student, program, and outcome variances.

Third, *summer school programs have more positive effects on the achievement of middle-class students than on students from disadvantaged backgrounds.* Students from middle-class families showed more positive effects of summer school, ranging from $d = .44$ to .56, depending on model assumptions and effect size adjustment, than students from disadvantaged backgrounds, ranging from $d = .20$ to .24. The difference between the economic groups was significant whether or not $d$-values were adjusted for methodological confounds and whether fixed-effect or random-effect assumptions were used to model error variance. In addition, the study by Heyns (1978) of Atlanta's large summer program with multiple goals revealed clear evidence for the moderating effect of student SES, but this study was not included in the meta-analysis of remedial programs.

We might speculate that the availability of more resources for middle-class families supplements and supports the activities occurring in the classroom in ways that may augment the impact of the summer program. Because such resources are available also to middle-class students who do not attend, however, this difference would have to exist as an interaction between attendance and resources, not a main effect of resources. Alternatively, summer programs in middle-class school districts may have better resources available, leading to smaller classes or more parent involvement. Heyns (1978) suggested that SES differences in summer school outcomes might occur because "programs are less structured and depend on the motivation and interest of the child" (p. 139). Finally, the learning problems of disadvantaged youth may be simply more intransigent than the problems of middle-class students.

Whatever the explanation, it is clear that, again to quote Heyns (1978), "the provision of educational resources is not sufficient to guarantee equal use or equal benefit" (p. 139). Although this point is valid, we also should emphasize three other points. First, even though the effect was larger for middle-class students, all four estimates of summer school's impact on disadvantaged students were significantly different from $d = .00$. Also, the few evaluations of summer programs for children of migrant workers indicated these programs had clear positive effects. And finally, if summer programs are targeted specifically at disadvantaged students they can serve to close the gap in educational attainment. Title I programs are of such nature.

Fourth, *remedial summer programs have larger positive effects when the program is run for a small number of schools or classes or in a small community.* We found that the size of the community and the number of schools and classrooms all revealed results that favored smaller programs, although the finding was not robust across our most conservative analytic permutations. Further, even the largest programs showed positive average effects that were significantly different from $d = .00$ for all analyses.

Based on these results, we speculate that the size-related program characteristics may be serving as proxies for associated differences in local control of programs and the specification and efficiency of program delivery that comes with local control. That is, small programs may give teachers and administrators greater flexibility to tailor class content and instruction to the specific needs of the students they serve and to their specific context. Small programs also may facilitate planning, and may remove roadblocks to the efficient use of resources. As our narrative descriptions of the literature suggested, among the reasons cited by teachers and parents for the failure of summer programs were last minute decision-making and untimely arrival of needed materials. These problems may be more prevalent when programs are large. As a caution to this interpretation, we should point out that the size-related program variables might also be related to the socioeconomic background of the community being served, with larger programs serving poorer communities. If this is the case, then economics might be the underlying causal factor, not local control.

Fifth, *summer programs that provide small group or individual instruction produce the largest impact on student outcomes.* The positive effect of individualized instruction was robust across all our analytic strategies, although significant class-size effects were restricted to fixed-effect analyses, suggesting it applies only to programs similar to those represented in our database. The reports explicitly stating that instruction occurred in small groups or one-on-one were among those that produced the largest effects of summer programs. Furthermore, those evaluations that solicited comments from teachers about the positive aspects of summer school often suggested that small group and individual instruction were among the program's strengths. We see no reason why the more general educational literature showing a relation between class size and achievement ought not apply to summer programs as well (Glass & Smith, 1979; Mosteller, 1995).

In addition to these principal conclusions, there are five other inferences we think can be drawn from the research synthesis, but with less confidence. We will list these in order of our general sense of their trustworthiness.

First, *summer programs that required some form of parent involvement produce larger effects than programs without this component.* Although this finding was robust across all our analyses, we chose to place it among our more tentative findings, because only three reports explicitly stated that the program included a parent involvement component and, although large on average, their effect size estimates varied widely. Still, the broader literature on parent involvement suggests this ought to be a positive program component (Cooper, Lindsay, & Nye, in press; Epstein, 1992) as long as parents have the skills to carry out the roles assigned to them and do so in a constructive manner (Casanova, 1996). The types of parent involvement required in the summer programs that we reviewed, including conferences with teachers, observing their child in class, and reading at home, are certainly constructive and should be manageable by most parents.

Second, *remedial summer programs may have a larger effect on math achievement than on reading.* We base this conclusion largely on the results of our meta-analysis comparing reading and math measures taken as outcomes within the same program. We think this is a powerful technique for uncovering differential effects of any treatment program. Still, we have placed it among our more speculative findings, because the within-study difference was significant only under fixed-effect assumptions and because we did not find a corresponding reliable difference when we examined subject matter differences in the curricula of the summer programs.

It is possible to interpret this finding in relation to summer learning loss. Specifically, the meta-analysis of summer loss research (Cooper et al., 1996) revealed that students' achievement scores in math show more of a drop during summer than reading achievement scores. The reason for the difference in loss was attributed to the likelihood that practice in reading is more embedded in students' everyday environments outside of school than is practice in mathematics. If this is the case, then control students likely received less practice during summer in math than in reading. Thus, the difference in the experiences of control students may explain the difference in summer school effects.

By highlighting the finding that summer school may be more efficacious for math than reading outcomes, we do not want to leave the impression that promoting literacy is an unworthy goal of summer programs. Summer school has positive effects on reading as well as math. Furthermore, illiteracy is a strong predictor of negative social behavior in both children and adults. According to Adams (1991), 75% of unemployed adults, 85% of juveniles who appear in court, and 60% of prison inmates cannot read. Therefore, when making decisions about summer school, the importance of additional instruction for children struggling with reading should be considered simultaneously with the efficacy of summer programs for fostering math skills. It seems clear that summer program content should be targeted to specific subpopulations of students. We will return to this notion below.

In Figure 2, we have tried to visually integrate the results of this research synthesis and the earlier synthesis of summer learning loss (Cooper et al., 1996). The figure distinguishes between change in achievement over

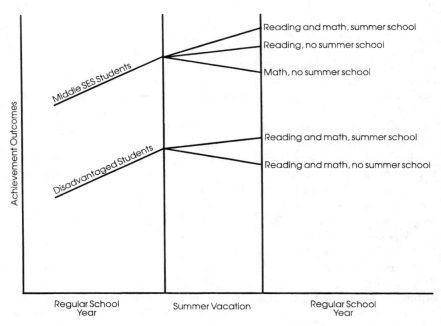

FIGURE 2.—Models of changes in achievement over summer as a function of student SES, subject areas, and summer school attendance

summer as a function of students' economic background and the subject matter. The models of learning over time refer to no specific grade level and make the more or less tenable assumptions that (a) middle-class students enter the model outperforming disadvantaged students (cf., McLoyd, 1998) but (b) there is little or no difference in the learning slopes of middle-class and disadvantaged students during the regular school year (cf. Entwisle & Alexander, 1992, 1994). Given these assumptions, the depicted achievement changes over summer reflect Cooper and colleagues' (1996) findings that (a) middle-class and disadvantaged students lose roughly equal amounts of math achievement over summer and (b) middle-class students gain somewhat in reading achievement over summer, whereas disadvantaged students lose reading achievement. Finally, the current findings are represented by summer school's positive effects on both reading and math achievement but somewhat more positive effect on the math achievement.

We offer the figure as a heuristic device and a work in progress. We hope the models are redrawn as knowledge accumulates concerning the effects of temporal patterns of schooling on achievement in different subject areas for different subpopulations of students using different instructional techniques. This knowledge would come, preferably, from the examination of interacting variables in individual studies, where researchers might ask, for example, "Is the differential effect of summer school on reading and math influenced by whether the student comes from a middle or low income family?" It also can be approached in meta-analysis by grouping studies based on two or more characteristics and examining differences in effect sizes, asking, for example, "Is the difference between reading and math effect sizes similar or different for samples of middle or low income students?" In meta-analysis, the search for interactions is often impeded (as it was for us) by few or no studies appearing in some cross-classification, for example, finding few effect sizes relating to summer school's influence on math skills of middle-class students. Meta-analysts also have to take care to pick which interactions to study based on credible theories or practical importance, because the number of potential interactions can be astronomical.

Third, *the achievement advantage gained by students who attend summer school may diminish over time.* Three of our four analyses revealed that measures with longer delays showed smaller effects. We would caution, however, against concluding that this finding indicates summer school effects are themselves not long-lasting. We uncovered multiple, subtle processes that might serve to obscure lasting effects. First, as pointed out by Klein and Gould (1970), students who do not attend summer programs may receive similar programs during the school year that are not made available to summer attendees. This can occur even when random assignment is used to choose participants, if nonparticipants are placed on a "waiting-list." Second, in nonequivalent group comparisons, when program participants are matched

HARRIS COOPER et al.

with nonparticipants after long delays, the match should be based on the students' status at the time of the program, not at the time of the delayed measurement. This procedure is necessary because changes in the matching status that occurred as a function of program participation and that are correlated with the delayed outcome (say, matching on absenteeism at the delayed time and then testing for achievement differences) would lessen the effect of the program. Finally, summer school may have positive effects on developmental trajectories that go unnoticed if students are not carefully matched. For example, remedial summer school might improve achievement or prevent summer learning loss while students attend, but these students might return to the preprogram trajectory after the program. In terms of Figure 2, this is akin to disadvantaged students having a lesser slope to their achievement gain during regular school sessions than middle-class students. If these students are compared to district averages at some later point, a comparison showing no program effect might obscure the existence of a halted or altered trajectory.

Fourth, *remedial summer school programs have positive effects for students at all grade levels, although the effects may be most pronounced for students in early primary grades and secondary school than in middle grades.* We had no a priori reason to expect such a curvilinear relationship. It proved significant, however, for fixed-effect analyses using effect sizes both unadjusted and adjusted for methodological confounds. Therefore, we will speculate that underlying the relationship may be the existence of three largely independent approaches to summer instruction associated with different grade levels. We base this speculation on Albuquerque Public Schools' (1985) description of the results of interviews of teachers following a summer program for all students. The interviews revealed elementary school teachers felt summer school gave them the opportunity to be more creative and to individualize instruction, middle school teachers said they emphasized study and organizational skills more than during regular session, and high school teachers, because of the credit structure, adhered most closely to regular session content. If these differences in approaches to summer school hold generally, we might expect the greatest achievement gains in the earliest and latest grades because it is here that teachers place the greatest emphasis on instruction in subject matter. Summer school in the middle years may place more emphasis on the teaching of subject-related study skills that eventually, but not immediately, have an impact on most outcome measures. Alternatively, it may simply be the case that summer school is most effective in the later grades because this is where the most summer loss takes place (Cooper et al., 1996).

Fifth, *summer programs that undergo careful scrutiny for treatment fidelity, including monitoring to insure that instruction is being delivered as prescribed, monitoring of attendance, and removal from the evaluation of students with many absences may produce larger effects than unmonitored programs.* All three indicators of treatment fidelity proved significantly associated with average effect sizes using fixed-effect but not random-effect assumptions and, therefore, these findings ought not be generalized beyond studies similar to those included in our database. These associations may be due to the impact that surveillance can have on the rigor with which programs are delivered. Or, they may simply indicate that the extra care that monitoring of programs implies is associated with other evaluation features, for example, care in data collection, related to the evaluation's likelihood of uncovering an effect.

Finally, two findings of the meta-analysis that deserve mention suggested inconsistent or a lack of mediation by student and program characteristic. First, *there is inconsistent evidence regarding whether or how the achievement label given to students is associated with the amount of benefit students derive from remedial summer programs.* Our two analyses using fixed-effect assumptions produced significant differences between achievement-label groups but the rank ordering of groups was not the same for unadjusted and adjusted *d*-indexes. Furthermore, neither random-effect analysis proved significant. As we noted in the introduction, one impetus for summer school is the federally mandated requirement that extended year services be available to children with disabilities who may suffer from regression of skills over the summer break (Public Law 94-142). Our results show clear and reliable benefits of summer school for these children, but these benefits appear relatively no greater in magnitude than the benefits for other students.

Second, *summer school remedial programs that require attendance appear no less effective, if not more effective, than programs that are voluntary.* Contrary to what we would have predicted, we found that programs identified as voluntary revealed smaller effects than programs that were nonvoluntary or that gave us no information on student choice. The finding was significant for both unadjusted and adjusted *d*-values, but using only fixed-effect assumptions for analysis. We thought that volunteering would serve as an indicator of motivation and engagement that would positively influence the impact of the summer program. Instead, it may be that compulsory attendance requirements are associated with student performance levels that are most likely to benefit from summer school activities. We are tentative, however, about this conclusion, because the programs we compared to the voluntary programs were not necessarily all nonvoluntary and our explanation for the findings is post hoc.

## INTERPRETING THE OVERALL EFFECT OF SUMMER SCHOOL

Our finding that summer school improves performance on outcome measures by about one seventh to one quarter of a standard deviation still leaves unanswered questions about how to interpret this effect. Is summer school an efficient strategy for educating students and meeting the broader needs of children and families? How does summer school compare to other interventions meant to improve the education of children and the well-being of children and families? To begin answering these questions, we need to devise a proper strategy for the interpretation of a quantitative effect.

One strategy is to express the magnitude of an effect in multiple metrics, ones that will provide different audiences with an intuitive sense of how large or small a particular effect is. For example, Cohen (1988) described a metric, $U_3$, that expresses an effect size in terms of the amount of overlap between two distributions. This metric tells us that when $d = .14$, the average person in the group with the higher mean outperformed about 55.6% of people in the group with the lower mean. When $d = .26$, $U_3$ equals about 60.2%. In the summer school case, then, we can say that the average child who attends a summer program will outperform between 55% and 60% of comparable students who did not attend the program.

In the section on effect size metrics, we introduced a set of guidelines provided by Cohen (1988) to help place effect sizes in context by providing some benchmark against which to evaluate their magnitude. Cohen defined a small effect as $d = .20$ and a large effect as $d = .80$. According to Cohen, then, the effect of summer school would be considered "small" when compared to all the behavioral sciences but "average" when compared to effects in fields allied with education and child development.

Cooper (1981) suggested a more comprehensive approach to effect size interpretation. Instead of a single criterion, he proposed the use of multiple contrasting elements as yardsticks. These should include some that (a) are broader than the treatment or predictor variable under consideration (e.g., how does the effect of summer school compare to other influences on achievement, including student family and community characteristics?), (b) are different from the treatment but within the same subclass (e.g., how does the effect of summer school compare to other educational interventions?), and (c) share the same treatment or predictor but vary in outcome measure (e.g., does summer school influence some spheres of learning more than others?). Cooper also suggested that effect sizes need to be interpreted in relation to the methodology used to generate them (e.g., the sensitivity of research designs, the trustworthiness of measures). Lipsey (1990) gives a similar approach to interpretation of effect sizes.

Today enough meta-analyses have been conducted that it is possible to find numerous related contrasting elements in the literature. For example, Walberg (1986) presented a list of 11 meta-analyses in education along with the average effect size obtained in each. The educational interventions and strategies on the list included programmed instruction, advanced organizers, and ability grouping, to name a few. The revealed effect sizes in these meta-analyses ranged from $d = -.12$ to .78. If we compare the findings of the summer school meta-analysis to these findings, it also suggests summer school had about an "average" impact on achievement.

Lipsey and Wilson (1993) presented a more recent and exhaustive compendium of meta-analyses. They compiled the results of 302 meta-analyses across the fields of education, mental health, and organizational psychology. The mean $d$-value across all these meta-analyses was $d = .50$. About three fourths of the 180 education meta-analyses revealed larger effects than did the summer school meta-analysis. Twenty-four meta-analyses of programs and techniques meant for remediation or to meet the needs of special students produced a range of $d$-values from $-.15$ to 1.04. Finally, after comparing the results of psychoeducational meta-analyses with others in the field of medicine, Lipsey and Wilson concluded "what does seem clear, however, is that in assessing meta-analytic estimates of the effects of psychological, educational, and behavioral treatment, we cannot arbitrarily dismiss statistically modest values (even 0.10 or 0.20 $SDs$) as obviously trivial" (p. 1199).

We would add to Lipsey and Wilson's caution another of our own. Just as primary studies use different methodologies that influence their outcomes, meta-analyses can use methods that are more or less conservative. There were two important decisions we made in conducting the summer school meta-analysis that would place our techniques among the more conservative when compared to other meta-analyses (but more reliable as well, we think). First, we included both published and unpublished reports in our meta-analysis. Other meta-analyses include only published reports and Lipsey and Wilson found that effect sizes gleaned from published reports were 36% larger than effects taken from unpublished reports. Second, our procedure of Winsorizing the most extremely positive effect sizes is still quite rare in meta-analysis.

Using a much narrower contrasting effect size, a meta-analysis conducted by Borman and D'Agostino (1996) examined the impact of regular school year Title I programs on the achievement of participants. These authors integrated the results of 17 federal summaries of local evaluations encompassing the test scores of over 41 million students. Their results, based largely on comparisons of students' preprogram and postprogram scores, revealed an average $d$-index of .11. This effect falls toward the lower end of our estimates of the effect of summer school. Differences in meta-analytic methodology, however, make categorical comparisons unwise. Still, it seems fair to conclude that the evidence suggests *summer remedial programs have no less of an effect on achievement than programs with similar goals conducted over the course of an entire regular school year.*

Also, there was remarkable consistency between the findings of our summer school meta-analysis and Borman and D'Agostino's Title I meta-analysis with regard to moderators of remedial program effects. Specifically, Borman and D'Agostino found that (a) control group comparisons yielded smaller effect sizes than pretest-postest comparisons, (b) regular-year remedial programs were more effective in lower grades, and (c) students in math programs tended to realize larger gains than students in reading programs. In addition, consistent with the summer learning loss literature, Borman and D'Agostino found that the summer break had detrimental effects on at-risk students, especially at-risk students in secondary school. This convergence of findings across independent meta-analyses of evaluations of different programs that share similar focuses and goals enhances the credibility of the conclusions of each.

Of course, judgments of "size" are not synonymous with judgments of "merit." The relative merit of different treatments involves considerations in addition to the magnitude of effect. Most critical among these would be (a) the cost of particular treatments and (b) the value placed on the changes the treatment is meant to create. Levin and colleagues have begun the task of establishing the relative cost-effectiveness of educational interventions (Levin, 1987; Levin, Glass, & Meister, 1987). They compared the cost-effectiveness of computer-assisted instruction, cross-age tutoring, reductions in class size, and increases in daily instructional time. First, they established an estimate of the magnitude of effect of each intervention over a constant treatment duration. Then, they calculated the cost per student of replicating each intervention. Finally, a cost-effectiveness ratio was established by calculating the effect size gain obtained for each $100 cost per student.

The information we currently have on summer school leaves such a cost-effectiveness comparison out of reach. We uncovered very few evaluations that included information on cost-per-pupil and most of these were out of date. Furthermore, because summer school can be configured in so many different ways, costs will vary dramatically depending on the components of the program. There are other complicating factors as well. For example, the nature of the interventions examined by Levin and colleagues would lead to widespread agreement that achievement measures provided the optimum, if not the sole, yardstick for judging each program's success. For summer school, although achievement is certainly a prime indicator of program success, advocates for summer programs also would call for the inclusion of other measures as indicators of success, such as reduced delinquency among adolescents and free, high-quality child supervision for poor families. We have seen that, to date, these measures are missing from the research literature. Still, it is important to recognize that from the perspective of the policymaker estimates of the relative cost-effectiveness of programs would be akin to the Holy Grail. They help make decisions about which programs to implement more scientific and less political.

## RECOMMENDATIONS FOR FUTURE RESEARCH TOPICS

Our recommendations for future research are based on three considerations. First, there is a need to uncover the causal mechanisms underlying some of the above-mentioned findings. We would hope that future researchers examine more closely the U-shaped relationship between summer program effects and grade level and the effect of student SES. We also think that the possible impact of local control on summer school outcomes is worthy of research resources.

Second, there is a need to replicate some of the more tentative findings, especially those associated with the moderating effects of voluntary versus nonvoluntary attendance and parent involvement. We would caution that studies of parent involvement be careful to distinguish between the impact of specific parent activities and the possibility that requiring parent involvement might select already involved parents into the program. Although either effect points to the importance of involved parents, only when the summer school requirement creates involvement that would not exist otherwise can we say that the program had its intended effect.

Third, the persistence of summer school effects over time is certainly an issue that requires greater attention. The investment of resources in summer programs is wasted if it does not result in lasting benefits for participating students. It is difficult to carry out multiple, long-term follow-up assessments of a program's effects. For political reasons, school districts can rarely wait years to produce evidence that a summer program works. Over time, programs lose funding or change in nature for reasons wholly unrelated to their educational effectiveness. Still, school districts should return and reassess their programs, even when the issue has fallen from the current policy radar screen. Long-term follow-ups can not only assess lasting benefits, but can look at different effects for multiyear and single-year attendees, can examine how programs during the school year interact with the summer school effect, and can chart changes in effectiveness as a function of changes in program delivery.

In addition, we think it would be profitable to pursue other possible influences on summer school effects that only rarely have been the topic of evaluation or were not robust predictors in our data set but which it may be premature to abandon at this point. Three of these are particularly interesting.

First and foremost, future research should expand the variety of outcome measures used to explore the impact of summer school. Research to date has rarely gone beyond the use of standard measures of academic achievement. Yet, the list of goals associated with summer school suggests many other possible outcomes. Even programs with primarily academic goals might find collateral effects that are of interest. We suggest special attention be paid to measures of student delinquency over summer, attitudes toward school, self-image, and attendance and discipline problems during the following school year, as well as broad indices of parent satisfaction and family interaction.

Of course, it is critical that when evaluators include multiple outcome measures, a clear distinction is made between those measures that are isomorphic with the primary goals of the program and those that measure collateral outcomes. Otherwise, program effects may appear smaller than is either desirable or anticipated. Related to our above discussion of the size of summer school effects relative to other interventions, we suspect that the average effect of summer school exhibited in this database suffers not insubstantially from many researchers measuring outcomes only tangentially related to program goals.

Second, the optimum length of summer programs appears to be an important topic for future investigation. The meta-analysis found no clear relationship between how long a summer program lasted and how successful it was. It seems reasonable to suggest that the optimum length of a program will interact with the goal of the program. For example, it may be that programs meant to deter juvenile delinquency will have optimum lengths that are longer than programs meant to teach specific subject content. The question of optimum length is important, because it has clear implications for the expenditure of resources. For example, if a program can be shortened and still reach its goals, then the program may be able to reach more students or do so in smaller groups while expending equal resources.

Third, as we found ourselves relating the summer school and summer learning loss literatures, we became increasingly intrigued by the possibility of a connection between positive summer school effects and the closeness of the last day of the summer program to the start of the next school year. We were not able to test this relation because few reports included the actual dates of the summer program and also employed a delayed measure of summer school effects. Applying a summer learning loss perspective suggests that programs immediately following the preceding school year ought to lose some of their benefit if students forget material in the weeks of vacation that follow. Programs that "back up" to the start of the new school year may be subject to less loss. The timing of summer school seems to have little impact on program costs, so this may be a very efficient way to enhance program outcomes. Possible negative effects on staffing and attendance, however, need to be considered. All the ramifications of scheduling are excellent topics for future study.

## RECOMMENDATIONS FOR FUTURE RESEARCH METHODOLOGY

Many of the program variations suggested in our recommendations for future research can rarely be achieved within a single evaluation. Most school districts implement a unified summer program in which variations in participants and delivery systems appear as unsystematic error. This pragmatic constraint highlights the value of research synthesis. Through the comparison of results across studies we can capitalize on program variations across sites to reach conclusions that are unobtainable otherwise. For research synthesis to be most effective, however, the primary evaluators must report the information needed by the next users of their data. Therefore, our first and strongest recommendation for future research methodology is for improved reporting standards for summer school evaluations.

We will not list all of the information that ought to be contained in a summer school evaluation report. Instead, we refer future evaluators to the previous description of our coding sheet. In the best case, all 93 of the reports would have included precise information on each of the 53 aspects concerning methodology, participants, programs, and outcomes. Long text descriptions would not be necessary, and might even be counterproductive for most evaluation agents who need to produce succinct reports for policy makers then move on to the next issue. A concise appendix with the appropriate information would suffice for research synthesis purposes. This practice would ensure that rather than informing only the immediate decision by a particular school district, the evaluation effort will inform other similar decisions that follow. Reciprocity would occur because all school districts would find an adequate database provided by others to help inform their next local decision.

Our second recommendation refers to how groups of students are formed to compare with summer school participants. We encourage evaluators to consider the use of random assignment whenever possible. We realize that experimental control often is impossible both practically and politically. The critical need for evaluations that possess the inferential strength of true experiments, however, should be obvious. The ambiguity associated with a lack of random assignment is the single greatest threat to the conclusions we have drawn from the summer school database. We did discover that the one-in-nine random-assignment sample comparisons revealed results consistent with those found in the less desirable designs. Still, the generally weak designs underlying this database remain a cause for concern.

Evaluators should keep an eye out for situations in which more children are eligible for summer school or volunteer to take part than can be accommodated by the program. When demand outstrips supply, an opportunity to conduct a lottery occurs and then tracking of lottery "winners" and "losers" reproduces the conditions of a randomized experiment.

Assignment should occur after students have expressed an interest in taking part in the program. If assignment occurs simply based on eligibility, then careful attention must be paid to refusal rates among students offered a summer school slot and refusers should be tracked along with students not invited. Cook and Campbell (1979) and Boruch (1998) address other problems that arise when conducting randomized experiments in field settings.

When random assignment is impossible, evaluators should consider using multiple comparison groups. Comparison groups matched by achievement, age, sex, race, SES, and/or achievement motivation are clearly preferable to unmatched district averages. And the more numerous the matching variables, the more confidence we can place in conclusions. Of these matching variables, motivation is clearly the most difficult to measure, as it often requires a testing done especially for the evaluation effort. Therefore, evaluators might consider a host of proxies for motivation that have rarely been used in previous studies, including prior attendance rate, participation in extracurricular activities, and discipline records.

Although district averages provide the most convenient comparison, we have seen that they often can give misleading results. Still, when certain characteristics of summer programs and participants are known, relative to a school district as a whole, we can make predictions about such comparisons that, if borne out, can enhance confidence in findings. Cohort analysis, in which students are compared to students from past years, can also be included in the same investigation as any of the other matching procedures.

Third, to reiterate a point made above, we would suggest that evaluators begin paying much more attention to cost analyses of summer schools. Per-pupil expenditures associated with the operation of summer programs, along with estimates of program effects, could provide invaluable information for policy makers who must decide between the relative effectiveness of two programs meant to accomplish the same goal. For example, assume a school district has instituted a policy that students will no longer be allowed to move on to the next grade unless they are reading at grade level. The district must then decide whether to provide a summer reading program to below-grade readers or to retain them in their current grade. During the 1st year of operation, the district finds that 50% of students in the summer program reached the grade-level criteria. In order to determine whether the program was cost-effective, the district compares the $2,000 cost per student of the summer program to the $6,000 cost per student of an additional school year. Under such constraints the program would be deemed cost-effective, because the "break even" point would be 33% of summer school students meeting the criteria.

Of course, this is a grossly oversimplified example. Tight educational budgets and calls for greater accountability concerning program cost-effectiveness dictate, however, that such estimates begin to be a part of the data regularly collected when we evaluate educational programs.

Fourth, we think there is an important place for qualitative research designs in summer school evaluations. For example, ethnographic studies of how summer school classes operate could shed much light on the grade-level differences uncovered in the meta-analysis. Case studies of children and families participating and not participating in summer programs could reveal many unexpected effects of programs, in terms of both behaviors that summer school fosters and behaviors that it replaces. Focus groups of students, parents, and teachers also could reveal latent effects as well as aspects of summer program design and delivery that might otherwise go unnoticed by evaluators.

Our final recommendation for research methodology concerns not *how* evaluations are conducted but *who* conducts them. Our results revealed that under fixed-effect assumptions evaluations conducted internally revealed effect sizes twice as large as evaluations conducted by external agents (although the effect all but disappeared when we used random-effect assumptions). One explanation for this finding is that internal evaluators may bias their studies in subtle, and not so subtle, ways because their own performance evaluations may be dependent on the program being deemed successful. Clearly, every precaution must be taken to avoid this threat to the integrity of evaluations, either through the hiring of external evaluators or other internal safeguards. Likewise, when external evaluators are used, they must be provided with thorough descriptions of program goals and implementation and unfettered access to the information they need to accomplish their task. This will not only protect against biased results, but will also ensure that the external evaluators do not underestimate the impact of programs because they did not know where or how to look for evidence that the program was having its intended effects.

## THE IMPLICATIONS OF RESEARCH FOR SUMMER SCHOOL POLICIES

We would like to conclude by offering some guidelines to policy makers and program implementers concerning the funding, development, and operation of summer schools. The guidelines are in no way inconsistent with the results of our research synthesis and most are based on them. On occasion, however, our proposals go beyond recommendations that have identifiable research underpinnings. When this occurs, we have drawn on inspiration gleaned from reading research reports along with district summer school materials, and from conversations with educators and others interested in summer school.

*Guidelines for policy makers.* Most obviously, *federal, state, and local policy makers should continue to fund summer school programs.* The research demonstrates that summer programs are effective at improving the academic skills of students taking advantage of them. Furthermore, summer school likely has positive effects well beyond those that have been measured in past research. Summer programs may inhibit delinquency among idle youth. They may prevent school failure for some students and therefore diminish future social costs associated with a lack of education. Also, as we argued in the Introduction, the need for summer programs will continue because of changes in family structure. Summer school appears to be a sound government and community response to meeting the needs of families and children created by the new American reality.

To ensure that summer programs are most effective and are accepted by the general public, *policy makers should require that a significant portion of funds for summer school be spent on instruction in mathematics and reading.* Because of the deeply engrained American mythos surrounding lazy summers, there is a tendency to accept summer school primarily for child care and guided recreation. Indeed, for single-parent families and for families in which both parents work outside the home, summer school will serve a child care function. For children who live in high crime and high poverty areas, summer programs will first and foremost provide safe and stimulating environments clearly preferable to the alternatives.

Both these goals are met regardless of the content of the program. We believe taxpayer acceptance of the additional expenditure of public funds required for summer school will be most directly tied to the program's ability to deliver educational benefit. Summer programs are proven effective vehicles to remediate, reinforce, and accelerate learning, and this opportunity should not be missed. We do not mean to imply that summer programs should not contain components relating to recreation and the arts. We do want to suggest that farsighted policy makers who earmark funds to ensure summer instruction in basic skill areas will win public support at the same time that they help dispel the cultural myth that schooling is a three-season activity.

*Policy makers should set aside funds for the specific purpose of fostering participation in summer programs, especially participation by disadvantaged students.* Summer programs often face serious problems in attracting students and maintaining their attendance. Summer programs are rarely mandatory and the consequences of nonattendance are remote. Summer programs compete for youthful attention with alternative activities that are often more attractive, but less beneficial. Even the most well-conceived program will fail if students choose not to enroll or attend. We think policy makers should earmark funds for transportation to and from summer programs and for food service at the program site. Comments in research reports as well as anecdotal evidence suggest providing these two services could greatly improve summer school enrollment and attendance. Visionary policy makers might even make provisions for siblings to attend summer programs so that parents will not keep older brothers and sisters home to provide child care for younger family members.

*Policy makers should offset the mandate for reading and math instruction by providing for significant local control concerning program delivery.* The research suggests the possibility that flexible delivery systems may lead to important contextual variations that significantly improve the outcomes of summer programs. Therefore, policy makers ought to resist the temptation to micromanage programs and give local schools and teachers leeway in how to structure and deliver programs.

Finally, *policy makers should require rigorous formative and summative evaluation of program outcomes.* Funds should be set aside for this specific purpose. Exactly how prescriptive policies requiring evaluation should be ought to depend on the funding mechanism (e.g., block versus competitive grants) and how distant the source of funds is from the operation of the program (e.g., federal versus local district mandates). Credible evaluations provide the accountability that is called for to justify expenditure of public funds. Also, although it always sounds self-serving for researchers to call for more funds for research, we hope that our attempt at integrating the research on summer schools has revealed both the benefits of research and the need for more credible research. Policy makers can make a substantial contribution to future data-based decision making by requiring and providing funds for systematic, ongoing program evaluation.

*Guidelines for program implementers.* There are numerous suggestions for implementation that can be gleaned from the research synthesis. For example, implementers should weigh the trade-off between the length of the program and the number of students served and how this trade-off is influenced by the program's goals. Implementers should consider ending programs close to the start of the new school year. Beyond the quantitative research results, some other suggestions were mentioned multiple times in the literature.

Surveys of teachers that accompany evaluations often point to a lack of planning time and late-arriving program materials as two of the most severe impediments to the success of a summer program. Thus, just as policy makers need to provide stable and continuing sources of funds for summer schools, program implementers need to plan early. We suspect that the pragmatics of program operation will take on a higher priority as summer schools are seen less as "add ons" and more as integral parts of the array of services provided by schools.

Related to planning is the need for program implementers to provide continuity from year to year. Priority for staffing should be based on past participation in the summer program itself so that teachers, administrators, aides, and support staff who took part in past years are given the first opportunity to be involved again. Evaluations should be used to continue successful elements of a program, from site locations to program content, and to discontinue unsuccessful ones.

Finally, program implementers also might consider integrating summer staff development activities for teachers with the teaching of summer school. The relatively small classes and relaxed atmosphere that many summer programs provide could make them an ideal laboratory for teachers to experiment with new curricula or pedagogical approaches. For example, teachers might learn about and discuss a new teaching strategy in the morning and then practice the approach using an afternoon summer school class. The coupling of staff development and summer teaching also might increase the pool of teachers interested in taking part.

*The Running Start summer program component.* As one example of how to break routine thinking about summer school, we would suggest educators consider a summer school program component we call the "Running Start." The guiding principle behind this component is that summer school can be profitably viewed as an extension of regular session instruction.

A Running Start component requires that the summer program be backed up against the new school year rather than follow immediately on the heels of the old year. The program need not occur immediately prior to the new school year, but the amount of interruption should be kept to a minimum. It also requires the participation of regular classroom teachers, although they need not be full-time summer instructors. In Running Start programs, regular class teachers might function as the resource teacher who pulls out students from the ongoing summer class routine.

Another key feature of Running Start is that teachers meet with, get to know, assess the strengths and weaknesses of, and begin instructing students who will be in their class when the new regular session begins. This strategy would seem most beneficial for students who are struggling in school, need special attention, or have the potential to present behavior problems when school begins. The length of the Running Start component could vary by local needs and resources.

Teachers should find that a running start with certain students more than compensates for their time, although additional pay should be provided as well. It will smooth the transition to the new school year by causing less time to be spent reviewing material when classes begin and, hopefully, diminishing disruptions caused by struggling students. These outcomes should benefit all class members, not just the program participants. As noted above, participation by teachers also could be incorporated into staff development opportunities to make the early return to school more attractive. Running Start students will benefit from extended instruction presented individually or in small groups and from the added sense of familiarity they achieve with their new teachers.

## CONCLUSION

The 9-month school calendar was adopted in America to accommodate the needs of a family-based, agrarian economy. In areas of the country where the 9-month school did not fit the economy, summer programs were quickly developed to prevent the negative social behaviors associated with idle youth. Educators soon discovered the potential of summer programs to improve learning. Summer education programs were viewed as especially attractive for children from homes with limited resources and for students with special learning needs.

In this synthesis, we have reexamined the evidence on the effectiveness of summer schools. Within the constraints of a less-than-optimal database, we have found summer school to be an effective system for attaining specific educational and social goals. Although the benefit varies according to characteristics of the child and program content and delivery, the generally positive effects of summer school for those who participate are unmistakable.

America's family structures are changing, its economy is diversifying, and its need is growing for all citizens to be educated well. All these forces dictate that we reexamine our myths about the seasonality of formal schooling.

# REFERENCES

Note: After each reference, an * indicates those studies included in the direction-only analysis and ** indicates those studies included in the meta-analysis.

Abram, M. J., & Cobb, R. A. (1979). *Evaluating a summer school program for elementary students achieving below grade level.* Bowling Green, KY: Professional Development Center Network. (ERIC Document Reproduction Service No. ED 197 971).**

Abram, M. J., & Maurelli, J. A. (1980). *Does attendance in summer school increase reading and math achievement of elementary students?* Owensboro, KY: PREPS Research Project. (ERIC Document Reproduction Service No. ED 209 269).**

Adams, M. J. (1991). *Beginning to read: Thinking and learning about print.* Cambridge, MA: MIT Press.

Agnew, A. T. (1975). *The effects of a summer communication skills program upon selected language arts skills and dimensions of the self concept of disadvantaged Negro pupils.* Unpublished doctoral dissertation, New Mexico State University, Las Cruces.*

Albuquerque Public Schools. (1985). *What I did instead of summer vacation: A study of the APS summer school program.* Albuquerque, NM: Albuquerque Public Schools. (ERIC Document Reproduction Service No. ED 281 932).

American Psychological Association. (1994). *Publication manual* (4th ed.). Washington, DC: Author.

Amorose, A. M. (1987). *Summer academic skills enhancement program, summer 1987. Final evaluation report.* Columbus, OH: Columbus Public Schools, Department of Evaluation Services. (ERIC Document Reproduction Service No. ED 296 058).**

Ascher, C. (1988). Summer school, extended school year, and year-round schooling for disadvantaged students. *ERIC Clearinghouse on Urban Education Digest, 42,* 1–2.

Ashton, B. D. (1983). *An evaluation of the process and product of the 1981 Let's Read summer school.* Unpublished doctoral dissertation, University of Michigan, Ann Arbor.**

Association of California School Administrators. (1988). *A primer on year-round education.* Sacramento, CA: Author.

Austin, G. R., Rogers, B. G., & Walbesser, H. H. (1972). The effectiveness of summer compensatory education: A review of the research. *Review of Educational Research, 42,* 171–181.

Barnett, V., & Lewis, T. (1978). *Outliers in statistical data.* Chichester, England: Wiley.

Barrett, M. J. (1990, November). The case for more school days. *The Atlantic Monthly,* 78–106.

Baxley, D. M., & Hinton, M. (1971). *The Eloy story: A report from the Eloy Elementary School summer migrant program for kindergarten through second grade level children.* Phoenix: Arizona State Department of Education. (ERIC Document Reproduction Service No. ED 067 217).**

Bergeth, R. L. (1975). *1975 Title I summer school program: An evaluation*. Minneapolis, MN: Research and Evaluation Department Planning and Support Services. (ERIC Document Reproduction Service No. ED 120 201).**

Borman, G. D., & D'Agostino, J. V. (1996). Title I and student achievement: A meta-analysis of federal evaluation results. *Educational Evaluation and Policy Analysis,* **18,** 309–326.

Boruch, R. F. (1998). Randomized controlled experiments for evaluations. In L. Bickman & D. J. Rog (Eds.), *Handbook of applied social research*. Thousand Oaks, CA: Sage.

Brody, L. E. (1984). *The effects of an intensive summer program on the SAT scores of gifted seventh graders*. Unpublished doctoral dissertation, Johns Hopkins University, Baltimore, MD.**

Brown, J. (1991, May). *A personalized reading approach for at-risk middle school students*. Paper presented at the Annual Meeting of the International Reading Association, Las Vegas, NV. (ERIC Document Reproduction Service No. ED 336 727).**

Burnes, J. (1985). *Colorado Migrant Education Program. 1983–1984 summary and evaluation report*. Denver: Colorado State Department of Education. (ERIC Document Reproduction Service No. ED 258 747).*

Campbell, D. T., & Stanley, J. C. (1966). *Experimental and quasi-experimental designs for research*. Chicago: Rand McNally.

Carroll, S. (1987). *The Connecticut summer incentive program: An evaluation of three years*. Torrington, CT: Bureau of Research and Evaluation. (ERIC Document Reproduction Service No. ED 300 470).*

Casanova, U. (1996). Parent involvement: A call for prudence. *Educational Researcher,* **25,** 30–32.

Chicago Public Schools. (1997). *Guidelines for promotion in the Chicago Public Schools*. Chicago: Chicago Public Schools.

Chmelynski, C. (1998). Higher standards create push for summer school. *School Board News,* **18**(4), 1, 12.

Cobb, S., Bonds, C., Peach, W., & Kennedy, D. E. (1990). Effectiveness of phonics for an intensive remedial program. *Reading Improvement,* **27,** 218–219.**

Cohen, J. (1988). *Statistical power analysis for the behavioral sciences*. Hillsdale, NJ: Erlbaum.

Conant, J. B. (1959). *The American high school*. New York: McGraw Hill.

Cook, T. D., & Campbell, D. T. (1979). *Quasi-experimentation: Design and analysis issues for field settings*. Chicago: Rand McNally.

Cooper, H. (1981). On the effects of significance and the significance of effects. *Journal of Personality and Social Psychology,* **41,** 1013–1018.

Cooper, H. (1998). *Synthesizing research: A guide for literature reviews*. Thousand Oaks, CA: Sage.

Cooper, H., & Hedges, L. B. (Eds.). (1994). *Handbook of research synthesis*. New York: Russell Sage Foundation.

Cooper, H., Lindsay, J. L., & Nye, B. (in press). Homework in the home: How student, family and parenting style differences relate to the homework process. *Contemporary Educational Psychology*.

Cooper, H., Nye, B., Charlton, K., Lindsay, J., & Greathouse, S. (1996). The effects of summer vacation on achievement test scores: A narrative and meta-analytic review. *Review of Educational Research,* **66,** 227–268.

Cramer, W., & Dorsey, S. (1969). A summer developmental reading program for rural students. *The Reading Teacher,* **22,** 710–713, 724.**

Culp, C. R. (1973). *An analysis of student achievement in arithmetic and reading as a result of summer school instruction in a selected Indiana city*. Unpublished doctoral dissertation, Indiana University, Bloomington.**

Curry, B. A. (1990). *The impact of the Nicholls State–Youth Opportunities Unlimited program as related to academic achievement, self-esteem, and locus of control*. Master's thesis, Nicholls

111

State University, Thibodaux, LA. (ERIC Document Reproduction Service No. ED 333 321).**

Curry, J. G., Griffith, J., Washington, W., & Williams, H. (1996). *Title I/Title I migrant evaluation report, 1995–96.* Publication Number 95.02. Austin, TX: Austin Independent School District. (ERIC Document Reproduction Service No. ED 405 447).*

D'Agostino, J., & Hiestand, N. (1995, April). *Advanced-skill instruction in chapter 1 summer programs and student achievement.* Paper presented at the meeting of the American Educational Research Association, San Francisco, CA. (ERIC Document Reproduction Service No. ED 390 929).**

Dailey, C. J. (1979). *Colorado Migrant Education Program. 1977–78 evaluation report. CDE evaluation series, No. 80-4.* Denver: Colorado State Department of Education. (ERIC Document Reproduction Service No. ED 192 979).*

David, J. L. (1974). *Summer study: A two-part investigation of the impact of exposure to schooling on achievement growth.* Unpublished doctoral dissertation, Harvard University, Cambridge, MA.**

DeLing, E. (1972). *In-depth evaluation of oral language instruction in the 1971 migrant education summer program.* Mount Pleasant, MI: Central Michigan University. (ERIC Document Reproduction Service No. ED 064 014).*

Donaldson, W. S. (1989). *Summer Academic Skills Enhancement Program. Final evaluation report.* Columbus, OH: Columbus Public Schools, Department of Evaluation Services. (ERIC Document Reproduction Service No. ED 319 860).*

Donaldson, W. S. (1990). *Summer Academic Skills Enhancement Program 1990.* Columbus, OH: Columbus Public Schools, Department of Evaluation Services. (ERIC Document Reproduction Service No. ED 327 608).*

Donaldson, W. S. (1992). *Fast track final evaluation report, Summer Academic Skills Enhancement Program.* Columbus, OH: Columbus Public Schools, Department of Evaluation Services. (ERIC Document Reproduction Service No. ED 354 286).*

Doss, D., Totusek, P., Curtis, J., Pankratz, C., Walker-Wheatley, K., Washington, W., & Shaw, L. (1979). Interim evaluation report: 1979 summer school program. Washington, DC: Department of Health, Education, and Welfare. (ERIC Document Reproduction Service No. ED 188 823).**

Dougherty, J. W. (1981). *Summer school: A new look.* Bloomington, IN: Phi Delta Kappa.

Entwisle, D. R., & Alexander, K. L. (1992). Summer setback: Race, poverty, school composition, and mathematics achievement in the first two years of school. *American Sociological Review,* **57,** 72–84.

Entwisle, D. R., & Alexander, K. L. (1994). Winter setback: The racial composition of schools and learning to read. *American Sociological Review,* **59,** 446–460.

Epstein, J. L. (1992). School and family partnerships. In M. Alkin (Ed.), *Encyclopedia of educational research.* New York: Macmillan.

Farley, R. (1996). *The new American reality.* New York: Russell Sage Foundation.

Fonzi, M. J. (1984). *The effect of summer school attendance on state student assessment test performance by grades three and five learning disabled students.* Unpublished doctoral dissertation, University of Florida, Gainesville.**

Fox, D. J., Harbatkin, L., MacDougal, R. L., Rosenzweig, L., Roth, W. J., & Storte, J. J. (1969). *1969 Summer day elementary school program for disadvantaged pupils.* New York: New York City Board of Education. (ERIC Document Reproduction Service No. ED 051 333).**

Fox, D. J., & Weinberg, E. (1967). *Summer schools for junior high and intermediate school pupils. Evaluation of New York City Title I educational projects, 1966–67.* New York: Center for Urban Education, New York Committee on Field Research and Evaluation, City College Research. (ERIC Document Reproduction Service No. ED 197 971).**

Franklin, M. L. (1987). *The effect of an eight-week summer school program on reading performance of severely emotionally disturbed students.* Unpublished doctoral dissertation, Southern Illinois University, Carbondale.\*\*

Garofalo, V. J. (1968). *Evaluation of migrant summer school programs supported by the New York State Department of Education during 1968. Final report.* Albany: New York State Education Department. (ERIC Document Reproduction Service No. ED 026 162).\*\*

Geis, R. (1968). *A preventive summer program for kindergarten children likely to fail in first grade reading.* La Canada, CA: La Canada Unified School District. (ERIC Document Reproduction Service No. ED 029 427).\*\*

Glass, G. V., & Smith, M. L. (1979). Meta-analysis of research on the relationship between class size and achievement. *Educational Evaluation and Policy Analysis, 1,* 2–16.

Godon, R. M. (1966). *Evaluation of 1966 EOA secondary summer school program. Research report.* Oakland, CA: Oakland Public Schools Research Department. (ERIC Document Reproduction Service No. ED 018 512).\*

Gousha, R. P. (1968). *Elementary summer school.* Milwaukee, WI: Milwaukee Public Schools. (ERIC Document Reproduction Service No. ED 028 212).\*\*

Greenhouse, J. B., & Iyengar, S. (1994). Sensitivity analysis and diagnostics. In H. Cooper & L. V. Hedges (Eds.), *The handbook of research synthesis.* New York: Russell Sage Foundation.

Hansen, J. B., Yagi, K., & Williams, G. L. (1986). *Elementary summer school, 1985 program in the Portland Public Schools.* Portland, OR: Portland Public Schools Department of Research, Evaluation. (ERIC Document Reproduction, Service No. ED 273 662).\*

Hayes, E. M., & Kerr, T. H. (1970). *An inter-disciplinary evaluation of a summer program for the rural disadvantaged youth in Nelson County, Virginia. Final report.* Washington, DC: Office of Education, Bureau of Research. (ERIC Document Reproduction Service No. ED 046 599).\*\*

Hedges, L. V., & Olkin, I. (1985). *Statistical methods for meta-analysis.* Orlando, FL: Academic Press.

Hedges, L. V., & Vevea, J. L. (1998). Fixed and random effects models in meta-analysis. *Psychological Methods, 3,* 486–504.

Heyns, B. (1978). *Summer learning and the effects of schooling.* New York: Academic Press.\*\*

Heyns, B. (1986). *Summer programs and compensatory education: The future of an idea.* New York. (ERIC Document Reproduction Service No. ED 293 906).

Hyman, J. E. (1988). *The effects of a remedial six-weeks summer school program on the achievement in and attitude toward reading and mathematics in grades four through eight.* Unpublished doctoral dissertation, University of South Carolina.\*\*

Karnes, F. A., Meriweather, S., & D'Llio, V. (1987). The effectiveness of the leadership studies program. *Roeper Review, 9,* 238–240.\*\*

Kashmuk, J., & Yagi, K. (1985). *Summer school 1984 program in the Portland Public Schools. 1983-84 evaluation report.* Portland, OR: Portland Public Schools. Research and Evaluation Department. (ERIC Document Reproduction Service No. ED 255 551).\*

Klein, E. B., & Gould, L. J. (1970). *Evaluation of the Yale summer high school: An experimental demonstration program of compensatory education for disadvantaged high school students. A two year follow up and evaluation.* New Haven, CT: Yale University. (ERIC Document Reproduction Service No. ED 047 082).\*\*

Klibanoff, L. S., & Haggart, S. A. (1981). *Technical report #8 from the study of the sustaining effects of compensatory education on basic skills.* Mountain View, CA: RMC Research Corporation. (ERIC Document Reproduction Service No. ED 213 789).\*\*

Kolloff, P. B., & Moore, A. D. (1989). Effects of summer programs on the self-concepts of gifted children. *Journal for the Education of the Gifted, 12,* 268–276.\*\*

Kulieke, M. J. (1986). Research design issues in the evaluation of programs for the gifted: A case study. *Journal for the Education of the Gifted, 9,* 193–207.\*\*

113

Levin, H. M. (1987). Cost-benefit and cost-effectiveness analysis. *New Directions for Program Evaluation*, **34**, 83–99.

Levin, H. M., Glass, G. V., & Meister, G. R. (1987). Cost-effectiveness of computer-assisted instruction. *Evaluation Review*, **11**, 50–72.

Leviton, H. S. (1973). *The effect of a summer compensatory education program on academic achievement and self-concept of primary grade learning disabled children with follow-up study.* Unpublished doctoral dissertation, University of Iowa, Iowa City.**

Lipsey, M. W. (1990). *Design sensitivity: Statistical power for experimental research.* Newbury Park, CA: Sage.

Lipsey, M. W., & Wilson, D. B. (1993). The efficacy of psychological, educational, and behavioral treatment. Confirmation from meta-analysis. *American Psychologist*, **48**, 1181–1209.

Lynch, S. J. (1992). Fast-paced high school science for the academically talented: A six-year perspective. *Gifted Child Quarterly*, **36**, 147–154.*

Mangino, E., & Ligon, G. (1983). *State Compensatory Education Summer School Program: 1982. Final evaluation report.* Austin, TX: Austin Independent School District, Office of Research and Evaluation. (ERIC Document Reproduction Service No. ED 235 231).*

Martin, V., Martin, R., & Hapeman, L. (1978). College preparatory program for visually impaired students: An evaluation. *Visual Impairment and Blindness*, **72**, 55–58.*

McDaniel, C., & Davis, A. (1989). *West Virginia Department of Education governor's Summer Youth Enhancement Program.* Charleston, WV: West Virginia State Department of Education. Bureau of Vocational, Technical, and Adult Education. (ERIC Document Reproduction Service No. ED 317 783).*

McLoyd, V. C. (1998). Socioeconomic disadvantage and child development. *American Psychologist*, **53**, 185–204.

McNeeley, S. (1996). *Title VII Special Alternative Grant Summer School: Literacy in Math and Science Project evaluation 1994–1995.* Cicero, IL: Cicero Board of Education. (ERIC Document Reproduction Service No. ED 397 080).*

Menousek, P. E. (1983). *An analysis of the factors affecting regression and recoupment of skills of special education students following summer vacation.* Unpublished doctoral dissertation, University of Nebraska, Lincoln.**

Merkel-Keller, C. (1987, April). *At what price success?—Summer basic skills remediation and paid employment.* Paper presented at the meeting of the American Education Research Association, Washington, DC. (ERIC Document Reproduction Service No. ED 281 998).**

Miller, R. C., Berney, T. D., & Mulkey, L. (1987). *E.C.I.A. Chapter 1 reading and math with athletics. Summer 1986.* New York: New York City Public Schools, Office of Educational Assessment. (ERIC Document Reproduction Service No. ED 298 195).**

Moss, J. R. (1988). *Utah migrant education annual summer evaluation report, 1988.* Salt Lake City: Utah State Office of Education. (ERIC Document Reproduction Service No. ED 309 020).*

Moss, J. R., & Griffen, B. (1986). *Utah migrant education annual summer evaluation report, 1986.* Salt Lake City: Utah State Office of Education. (ERIC Document Reproduction Service No. ED 280 669).*

Mosteller, F. (1995). The Tennessee study of class size in early school grades. *Future of Children*, **5**(2), 113–127.

National Commission on Excellence in Education. (1983). *A nation at risk: The imperative for educational reform.* Washington, DC: U.S. Department of Education.

New York City Board of Education (1992). *Chapter 1–funded summer programs: Institute for Career Exploration (ICE), the Basic Skills Programs, the Basic Reading Program, and Project YOU (Youth Opportunities Unlimited). OREA report.* Brooklyn, NY: Office of Research, Evaluation, and Assessment. (ERIC Document Reproduction Service No. ED 357 128).*

North Carolina State Department of Public Instruction. (1988). *Report of student performance: The 1987 Basic Education Program Summer School.* Raleigh: North Carolina State Department of Public Instruction. (ERIC Document Reproduction Service No. ED 295 949).*

Oliphant, L. A. (1988). *A two-year analysis of the relationship between summer school participation and non-participation and the reading and mathematics achievement of primary school children.* Unpublished doctoral dissertation, University of San Francisco.**

Olszewski, P., Kulieke, M. J., & Willis, G. B. (1987). Changes in the self-perceptions of gifted students who participate in rigorous academic programs. *Journal for the Education of the Gifted,* **10**, 287–303.**

Opuni, K. A., Tullis, R., & Sanchez, K. S. (1990). *Beating the Odds Summer School: A dropout prevention program for at-risk students (1990).* Houston, TX: Houston Independent School District. (ERIC Document Reproduction Service No. ED 327 628).**

Ouellette-Howitz, J., & Murray, T. (1998). *Annual report to the Board of Education, Minneapolis Public Schools.* Minneapolis, MN: Minneapolis Public Schools. Unpublished manuscript.*

Overton, R. C. (1998). A comparison of fixed-effects and mixed (random-effects) models for meta-analysis tests of moderator variable effects. *Psychological Methods,* **3**, 354–379.

Petro, J. R., Pimentel, D. C., Hinkle, B., Burnes, J., & Stewart, D. (1993). *On the move: Migrant education 1991–92.* Denver: Colorado State Department of Education, Planning and Evaluation Unit. (ERIC Document Reproduction Service No. ED 364 383).*

Petro, J. R., Pimentel, D. C., Hinkle, B., Burnes, J., & Stroup, K. (1994). *On the move: Migrant education 1992–93.* Denver: Colorado State Department of Education. (ERIC Document Reproduction Service No. ED 383 500).*

Pfeifer, J. D. (1985). *Student accountability and course repetition: What works best?* Master's thesis, Southern Oregon State College, Ashland. (ERIC Document Reproduction Service No. ED 272 450).*

Porterfield, C., & Eglasaer, R. (1980). *Technical report: 1979–80 ESAA Basic Summer School.* Austin, TX: Austin Independent School District, Office of Research and Evaluation. (ERIC Document Reproduction Service No. ED 193 623).**

Rachel, J. (1987). *Student placement study: 1985–86 state-funded compensatory/remedial program evaluation.* Baton Rouge: Louisiana State Department of Education. (ERIC Document Reproduction Service No. ED 269 445).*

Rawson, H. E. (1992). Effects of intensive short-term remediation on academic intrinsic motivation of "at-risk" children. *Journal of Instructional Psychology,* **19**, 274–285.**

Rawson, H. E. (1993). Academic gain in maladjusted children. *Therapeutic Care and Education: The Journal of the Association of Workers for Children with Emotional and Behavioral Difficulties,* **2**, 392–403.**

Richardson, J. B. (1968). *Evaluation of Roosevelt Junior High School summer demonstration program.* Oakland, CA: Oakland Public Schools. (ERIC Document Reproduction Service No. ED 017 568).*

Richmond, M. J. (1977). *Issues in year-round education.* Hanover, MA: Christopher Publishing House.

Robbins, E. L., & Thompson, L. W. (1989). *A study of the Indianapolis–Marion Ccounty Public Library's summer reading program for children: Final report.* Indianapolis, IN: Indiana University–Purdue University. (ERIC Document Reproduction Service No. ED 316 845).*

Robbins, E. L., & Thompson, L. (1991). *A study of the Indianapolis–Marion County Public Library's summer reading program for children.* Indianapolis, IN: Measurement and Evaluation Center in Reading Education. (ERIC Document Reproduction Service No. ED 335 647).*

Roderick, S. A., Hansen, L., & Inwood, B. H. (1979, April). *Evaluation of a successful remedial summer school program.* Paper presented at American Educational Research Association

1979 Annual Meeting, San Francisco, CA. (ERIC Document Reproduction Service No. ED 171 798).*

Rose, J., Pimentel, D. C., Hinkle, B., Burnes, J., Stewart, D., & Randall, W. T. (1992). *On the move: Migrant education 1990–91.* Denver: Colorado State Department of Education. (ERIC Document Reproduction Service No. ED 353 097).*

SAS Institute. (1985). *SAS user's guide: Statistics* (Version 5). Cary, NY: Author.

Seever, M. L. (1991). *The summer school program, 1991: Summative evaluation.* Kansas City, MO: Kansas City School District. (ERIC Document Reproduction Service No. ED 346 966).*

Shapiro, J. Z. (1986). *LSYOU (Lousiana State Youth Opportunities Unlimited): Project evaluation.* Baton Rouge: Lousiana State University, College of Education. (ERIC Document Reproduction Service No. ED 275 815).*

Siegelman, M. (1975). *Summer mathematics remediation for incoming pupils: 1975 high school umbrella #2.* New York: Board of Education of the City of New York, Office of Educational Evaluation. (ERIC Document Reproduction Service No. ED 138 661).**

Sipe, C. L. (1986). *Summer Training and Education Program (STEP): The experience of Hispanic participants in the summer of 1985.* Philadelphia: Public/Private Ventures. (ERIC Document Reproduction Service No. ED 286 697).*

Sipe, C. L., Grossman, J. B., & Milliner, J. A. (1987). *Summer Training and Education Program (STEP): Report on the 1986 experience.* Philadelphia: Public/Private Ventures. (ERIC Document Reproduction Service No. ED 283 027).*

Sipe, C. L., Grossman, J. B., & Milliner, J. A. (1988). *Summer Training and Education Program (STEP): Report on the 1987 experience.* Philadelphia: Public/Private Ventures. (ERIC Document Reproduction Service No. ED 300 479).**

Slavin, R. E. (1986). Best-evidence synthesis: An alternative to meta-analytic and traditional reviews. *Educational Researcher, 15,* 5–11.

Smith, C. M. (1972). *An exploratory study of the effects of compensatory education on the reading and mathematics achievement of intermediate grade pupils.* Paper presented at the meeting of the American Educational Research Association, Chicago, IL. (ERIC Document Reproduction Service No. ED 065 602).

Smith, F. L. (1992). *Nature-Computer Camp 1991: Chapter 2 program evaluation report.* Washington, DC: District of Columbia Public Schools. (ERIC Document Reproduction Service No. ED 352 345).*

Steinmiller, G., & Duncan, L. B. (1991). *Arkansas Youth Opportunities Unlimited Follow-Up. Final report.* Arkadelphia, AR: Henderson State University. (ERIC Document Reproduction Service No. ED 361 555).*

Steinmiller, G., & Steinmiller, R. (1993). *Youth Opportunities Unlimited: The results of a three year study.* Arkadephia, AR: Henderson State University. (ERIC Document Reproduction Service No. ED 358 996).*

Stevenson, H. W., & Lee, S. (1990). Contexts of achievement. *Monographs of the Society for Research in Child Development, 55* (1–2), Serial No. 221.

Strike, K., & Posner, G. (1983). Types of syntheses and their criteria. In S. Ward & L. Reed (Eds.), *Knowledge structure and use: Implications of synthesis and interpretation.* Philadelphia: Temple University Press.

Taggert, J. B., Mecham, S. K., & Ortega, J. (1991). *Utah migrant education annual summer evaluation report.* Salt Lake City: Utah State Office of Education. (ERIC Document Reproduction Service No. ED 244 726).*

Tam, H. P. (1987). *CLEAR–Reading Recovery Summer Project, summer 1987.* Columbus, OH: Columbus Public Schools, Department of Evaluation Services. (ERIC Document Reproduction Service No. ED 290 126).**

Texas Education Agency. (1982). *Report on ESEA, Title I migrant, 1980–81 (Texas).* Austin, TX: Texas Education Agency. (ERIC Document Reproduction Service No. ED 218 040).*

Thompson, D. R. (1989). *Metro Achievement Program summer 1988. External evaluation report.* (ERIC Document Reproduction Service No. ED 317 651).**

Toledo, V. (1975). *Summer reading remediation for incoming pupils 1975 high school umbrella #2.* New York: Board of Education of the City of New York, Office of Educational Evaluation. (ERIC Document Reproduction Service No. ED 137 441).**

Trangmoe, J. (1988). *Glendive Migrant Program. Dedicated to meeting the needs of migrant children and their families.* Helena: Montana State Department of Public Instruction. (ERIC Document Reproduction Service No. ED 317 333).*

Tukey, J. W. (1977). *Exploratory data analysis.* Reading, MA: Addison-Wesley.

Tyler, J. W. (1966). *Human development project.* Richmond, VA: Richmond City School Board and The Ford Foundation. (ERIC Document Reproduction Service No. ED 018 493).**

Walberg, H. J. (1986). Syntheses of research on teaching. In M. C. Wittrock (Ed.), *Handbook of research on teaching* (3rd ed.). New York: Macmillan.

Ward, M. S. (1989, March). *North Carolina's summer school program for high-risk students: A two-year follow-up of student achievement.* Paper presented at the Annual Meeting of the American Educational Research Association, San Francisco, CA.**

Wasik, B. H., & Sibley, S. A. (1969). *An experimental summer kindergarten for culturally deprived children.* Durham, NC: Duke University. (ERIC Document Reproduction Service No. ED 044 174).**

Welch, M., & Jensen, J. B. (1990). Write, P.L.E.A.S.E.: A video-assisted strategic intervention to improve written expression of inefficient learners. *Remedial and Special Education, 12,* 37–47.**

Wells, D. H., Springer, T. P., & McCready, M. A. (1987). *Curbing dropout rates: An ecological model.* Louisiana Tech University, Ruston. (ERIC Document Reproduction Service No. ED 296 072).**

White, K. (1998). The heat is on as big districts expand summer school. *Education Week, 17*(42), 7.

Williams, M. T. (1977). *Summer school attendance and the retention of reading skills of selected fourth grade students.* Unpublished doctoral dissertation, Louisiana State University, Baton Rouge.**

Winston, C. M. (1963). *Meeting needs of gifted: A non-structured summer program: 1962–1963 school year.* Albany: State University of New York. (ERIC Document Reproduction Service No. ED 039 674).**

Woloshin, G. W. (1975). *College Bound Program, summer 1975.* New York: Board of Education of the City of New York, Office of Educational Evaluation. (ERIC Document Reproduction Service No. ED 135 918).**

Womble, M. L. (1977). *Summer recess: Does it make a difference on Title I student achievement?* (ERIC Document Reproduction Service No. ED 141 445).**

Worsnop, R. L. (1996). Year-round schools: Do they improve academic performance? *CQ Researcher, 6,* 433–456.

Yinger, J. M., Ikeda, K., & Laycock, F. (1970). *Middle start supportive interventions for higher education among students of disadvantaged backgrounds.* Oberlin, OH: Oberlin College. (ERIC Document Reproduction Service No. ED 047 659).*

# ACKNOWLEDGMENTS

This research was support by a grant from the U.S. Department of Education, National Institute on the Education of At-Risk Students (R306F60041-97). The opinions expressed herein are those of the authors and not necessarily the funding agency. Thanks are extended to Linda Coutts, Cyndi Kernahan, Barbara Nye, and Kim Ratcliff for assistance with data collection and manuscript preparation. Correspondence concerning this article may be addressed to Harris Cooper, Department of Psychology, McAlester Hall, University of Missouri, Columbia, MO 65211; phone: (573) 882-3360; email: cooperh@missouri.edu.

THE EFFECTS OF SUMMER SCHOOL:
QUESTIONS ANSWERED, QUESTIONS RAISED

*Geoffrey D. Borman*

This *Monograph* makes important contributions at two levels: first, as an impressive methodological model of a combination of useful and under-utilized meta-analytic techniques, and second, as an unprecedented quantitative synthesis of substantive research on the effects of summer school. The authors were faced with the challenge of making sense of the results from primary studies that differed in terms of the (a) reports themselves (e.g., journal article, dissertation, external evaluation, or internal evaluation); (b) methods (e.g., pretest-posttest comparison, experimental comparison, or nonequivalent control-group design); (c) student samples (e.g., at-risk, average, or gifted students); (d) actual characteristics of the summer programs (e.g., remediation or enrichment); and (e) indicators of the summer program's effectiveness (e.g., teacher-constructed or standardized tests). Differences such as these are commonly found in the social sciences, especially in the case of education. Nevertheless, some analysts have chosen to pool findings from primary studies of somewhat different methodologies and varying relevance to the issue at hand, while others, using highly restrictive criteria for the inclusion of primary studies, simply choose to omit large chunks of the literature. Cooper and colleagues' methods exemplify not only how one may account for these differences when determining an overall estimate of the summer school effect, but also how one may take advantage of this natural variation across studies to discover how educators can—as the title of their *Monograph* suggests—make the most of summer school. This approach simultaneously responds to important criticisms of traditional meta-analytic methods, such as those of Slavin (1986), and draws together policy-relevant summative and formative conclusions regarding a complicated research base.

119

In the pages that follow, I present a brief discussion of the notable questions this study answers and of some of the questions that it raises. I begin by summarizing the methodological contributions of the *Monograph*, and by emphasizing a few of the more important lessons that meta-analysts may learn from this work. Second, I situate this work in the literatures on summer learning and on education for poor and minority children and discuss the potential for summer school to advance educational equality. I conclude by suggesting where additional research is needed to close gaps in both the summer learning and summer school research bases.

## Methodological Contributions

Varying perspectives exist on what the synthesist should do about differences across primary studies in terms of overall research quality and other features, such as the research designs, samples, and the actual circumstances involved. For instance, on one hand, Glass (1976) stated, "it is an empirical question whether relatively poorly designed studies give results significantly at variance with those of the best designed studies" (p. 4). On the other hand, Slavin (1986) argued, "far more information is extracted from a large literature by clearly describing the best evidence on a topic than by using limited journal space to describe statistical analyses of the entire methodologically and substantively diverse literature" (p. 7). Should one combine studies that have varying methods and varying substantive characteristics or should one focus only on the "best evidence"?

In truth, the answer probably depends most on the meta-analyst's research questions. If one wants to know the effect of a treatment applied for at least 3 weeks based on data from only the most rigorous experimental studies, then the analyst should choose the small number of studies that fit that description. If one is interested in studying how much the effect varied depending on treatment duration, and in assessing the difference in effect estimates from experimental and quasi-experimental studies, however, then the analyst may learn considerably more by systematically investigating the variance in effect-magnitude parameters across a group of studies that differ along these dimensions. The most important questions of Cooper and his colleagues are similar to those referred to in the latter case. Specifically, the authors assumed a priori that the summer programs to be included in their synthesis would vary, and that the research methods for studying these summer programs would vary. Indeed, when hypothesizing about the potential differences in effect estimates associated with the numerous identifiable (and unidentifiable) programmatic and methodological variations noted in the summer school literature, the authors stated that "most of the multitude of permutations and interacting influences have no or few empirical testings noted in the research literature"(p. 17). This multitude of potential moderators underlies the concept of a true effect size as random. As Raudenbush (1994) pointed out, the concept of randomness arises from the belief that the outcome of a process cannot be predicted in advance, precisely because the sources of influence on the outcome are both numerous and unidentifiable.

The ways in which Cooper and his colleagues dealt with this randomness, the numerous moderators of effect sizes, and the general complexities of this literature are exemplary. First, they contrasted underutilized (at least in the social sciences) random-effects analyses of their data with more conventional fixed-effects analyses. Second, they demonstrated a procedure for obtaining a rough estimate of the average effect size for a group of studies for which only the direction of the treatment effect was known. Third, the authors employed an infrequently used technique for adjusting effect sizes to remove the covariance between methodological and substantive characteristics. Fourth, they showed how an analyst may take advantage of subgroups of studies that contain substantively interesting variations within them. For instance, in looking at a subgroup of studies that measured both math and reading outcomes, the authors were able to draw stronger inferences about differential impacts of summer programs on math and reading achievement because most, if not all, other variations were held constant. Finally, in integrating narrative and quantitative techniques for research synthesis, the authors clearly outlined and discussed the complexities of this literature, and described how the known differences across the studies impacted summer school effect estimates. In this way, the authors productively utilized the variability across studies to qualify the conditions under which summer programs are more successful, and to quantify precisely how much more successful they are. None of these procedures is new, but their thoughtful integration is novel, instructive to the student of meta-analysis, and representative of how a complex literature such as this should be integrated and reported.

Through an exhaustive quantitative synthesis of the literature, Cooper and colleagues' methods provide the parsimony of the traditional meta-analysis, but they also clearly discuss, statistically account for, and productively model the various caveats of the individual studies. In reviewing an earlier version of this *Monograph*, I noticed that the authors had identified their methods—referring, most notably, to those that combined narrative and quantitative review—as unprecedented. I pointed out to the authors, however, that Slavin's (1986) ideas about best-evidence synthesis seemed to represent a precedent, which the authors graciously conceded in the final version of the *Monograph*. In a way, though, the authors' integration of narrative and meta-analytic methods is distinct from what Slavin had in mind. The authors did not limit their review to a somewhat homogeneous collection of the best evidence, as Slavin advised, but instead used procedures that enabled them to synthesize the entire methodologically and substantively heterogeneous literature. Therefore, rather than only the best evidence, Cooper and colleagues' methods applied narrative description to the larger literature, which, with all of its caveats, would seem to be the most likely candidate for thorough discussion. The authors have illustrated how the analyst may consider all of the evidence, and, through both statistical and narrative exposition, discover those studies that provide the best answers to two questions: What is the overall effect of summer school, and what are the features of summer programs most consistently associated with improved student outcomes?

## Substantive Contributions

Two important substantive contributions of the *Monograph* are the finding that summer school does, in fact, make a difference and the findings related to designing more effective programs. Previous narrative reviews by Austin, Rogers, and Walbesser (1972), Heyns (1986), and Ascher (1988) concluded that summer programs had only modest effects on student achievement and that the research evidence, in general, was limited. In contrast, based on evidence from 93 reports, Cooper and his colleagues computed an overall summer school effect of between one seventh and one quarter of a standard deviation. The authors' useful comparisons of this result to other related outcomes indicated that the impact of summer school on achievement is about the same as the "average" effect in the social sciences and is at least as strong as the effect of similar programs conducted over the regular school year.

Those interested in developing or refining summer programs will learn several important lessons from this *Monograph*. For instance, effective programs (a) involve parents, (b) undergo careful scrutiny for treatment fidelity, (c) contain substantial academic components aimed at teaching reading and math, and (d) coordinate summer school experiences with those that occur during the regular school year. The authors raised several other important caveats related to additional program characteristics and to the actual background characteristics of the students served by the programs. Although Cooper and colleagues reported that students from middle-class backgrounds showed larger achievement gains than students from disadvantaged backgrounds, all students were found to benefit from summer school. This finding, along with Cooper, Nye, Charlton, Lindsay, and Greathouse's (1996) prior conclusions related to low socioeconomic status (SES) students' summer learning losses, raises perhaps the most important implication of this work: the potential impact of summer school on improving educational opportunities and outcomes for disadvantaged children.

Indeed, the large and persistent achievement gaps between minority poor students and White middle-class students are enduring national problems. These gaps tend to separate advantaged and disadvantaged students when they begin their formal schooling, and a recent meta-analysis by Phillips, Crouse, and Ralph (1998) and the work of Alexander and Entwisle (1996) provide some evidence that the gaps also may expand as students proceed through school. What are the causes of these gaps, and what processes may account for their apparent widening? Differences in home resources, parenting practices, and in the availability and quality of preschool are some of the factors that appear to contribute to early achievement differences between poor minority and middle-class White children (Jencks & Phillips, 1998). The widening of achievement gaps as students proceed through school would seem, quite naturally, to implicate the schools and to lend support to the contentions of researchers such as Bowles and Gintis (1976) that schools magnify existing inequities by reinforcing outside sources of disadvantage. Data from Karl Alexander and Doris Entwisle's long-term Beginning School Study, however, suggest that the widening of the gaps is not explained by differential school-year learning rates, but by summer learning differences. Specifically, Alexander and Entwisle (1996) demonstrated that the significant achievement difference between disadvantaged and advantaged students that developed from elementary to middle school is almost entirely attributable to differences in gains made during summer vacations.

The combination of findings from this *Monograph* and from Alexander and Entwisle's Beginning School Study may have tremendous implications for educational equality. If summer learning differences, compounded year after year, are the primary cause of widening achievement gaps, could a series of yearly summer school programs for disadvantaged students prevent the gap from widening? In Figure 2 of their *Monograph*, Cooper and colleagues charted the 1-year effects of summer vacation and summer school on middle-SES and disadvantaged students' learning. Expanding upon this model, I depict in Figure 1 the hypothetical reading achievements of middle-SES and disadvantaged students across 4 summers and 5 school years. Like the findings of Alexander and Entwisle (1996), this figure illustrates the cumulative widening of the achievement gap between middle-SES and disadvantaged summer program nonattendees. Alternatively, expanding on Cooper and colleagues' findings for the 1-year effect of summer school, the figure suggests that disadvantaged students who are provided summer programs year after year are able to keep pace with the achievements of middle-SES students. To achieve absolute equality, additional interventions are needed, either to bridge the gap separating advantaged and disadvantaged students when they begin their formal schooling or to accelerate the school-year growth of disadvantaged students. If the repeated effect of

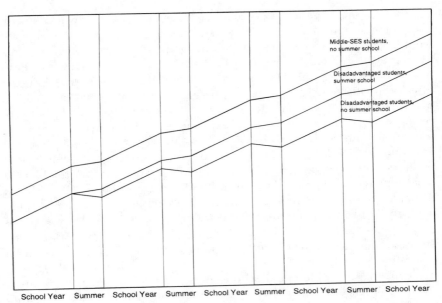

Middle-SES students, no summer school

Disadadvantaged students, summer school

Disadadvantaged students, no summer school

School Year Summer School Year Summer School Year Summer School Year Summer School Year

FIGURE 1.—A model of seasonal learning differences and summer school effects for disadvantaged students

summer school is similar to the 1-year effect found by Cooper and colleagues, however, summer school may be the primary intervention through which educators prevent the cumulative widening of the reading achievement gap.

### The Questions Raised

Because no known studies have examined the effects of multiyear summer school programs and because little (beyond Alexander and Entwisle's work with a sample of Baltimore students) is known about the cumulative effects of seasonal learning differences, the achievement trends displayed in Figure 1 remain largely hypothetical. To begin plotting these trends with greater confidence, we must begin with nationally representative studies of the longitudinal effects of seasonal learning differences. As the work of Cooper et al. (1996) demonstrated, summer learning losses vary by subject area and by skill area within subjects. Therefore, we must obtain good measures of both reading and math, but we also need precise measures of more specific skill areas, such as reading vocabulary and comprehension and math computation and conceptual application, in addition to overall reading and math scores. Studies of seasonal learning differences are vital for advancing the child development and educational equality fields, but because these studies require that we assess students twice a year (once during the fall and once during the spring), they are expensive and they place additional burdens on schools and students. Testing students once a year, though, is largely a waste of resources because it is impossible to disentangle summer and school-year differences in children's cognitive development.

We also have a lot to learn about summer school. First, if we want to prevent summer learning losses, it makes little sense to begin mandating summer school only after students have fallen behind in their *regular school year* work. Yet, that is how most large-scale summer school programs operate in places like Chicago, Denver, East Baton Rouge, Minneapolis, Norfolk, and Springfield (Massachusetts) (Chmelynski, 1998). To prevent summer learning losses, and possibly to accelerate regular school year development, we need proven, replicable programs that (a) begin in the early grades, (b) are offered over multiple summers, and (c) focus on prevention and development rather than remediation. Cooper and colleagues' exhaustive literature review testifies, however, that there are no summer school programs of any type that have been widely replicated and evaluated. Educators today have a variety of research-proven and replicable school-year interventions, such as Success For All and the Comer School Development Program, from which to choose. Those interested in implementing proven summer school programs should have similar options.

In addition to the significant development activities that are needed to build research-proven summer school programs, of course, we also need high-quality research. Whenever possible, programs should be evaluated using carefully designed randomized experiments. Random assignment typically is difficult to carry out in schools and classrooms. With popular voluntary summer programs, however, which have more applicants than seats available, it is relatively easy for evaluators to justify assignment by random lottery as a fair (and scientifically superior) process. Cooper and colleagues provided some very useful information regarding some of the characteristics of more successful interventions, but there are many other questions that remain unanswered. Some of the more important questions include: (a) What are the longitudinal effects of single-year programs? (b) What are the longitudinal effects of multiyear programs? (c) Does summer school accelerate regular school-year learning as well as summer learning? and (d) What types of programs are most effective for preventing summer learning losses?

Finally, in addition to conducting formative evaluations of students attending programs, surveys and qualitative studies of nonattendees who are at-risk for summer learning losses also may help us understand how to

125

develop effective programs. For example, naturally occurring comparisons between at-risk students who lose ground and at-risk students who are less affected by the summer vacation may help us gain a better understanding of the behaviors or individual characteristics that set these students apart. Aside from Heyns's (1978) findings that more successful summer learners did more reading and traveling alone, we know very little about the alterable student behaviors that are associated with improved summer learning outcomes.

Contemporary statistical techniques, most notably multilevel models, have helped educational researchers more accurately and efficiently partition and explain the contributions of schooling and families to students' cognitive development. The contrast, however, of summer learning, which reflects the influence of families in the absence of formal schooling, to school-year learning, which represents the interaction between family and school, offers a level of experimental control that goes beyond statistical adjustment. It was not long ago that the school-effects research contributed to a general sense of pessimism about the impacts of schools. More recently, though, studies of these seasonal variations in student learning have elegantly highlighted both the additive and the equalizing effects of schools. Specifically, all children grow at faster rates while in school and these in-school learning rates are far more equal than summer learning rates. Cooper and colleagues' work builds on this by demonstrating the ways in which schools may also advance and equalize summer learning rates. Based on this research, and based on additional research and development, we must implement proven programs to accomplish both of these goals.

## References

Alexander, K. L., & Entwisle, D. R. (1996). Early schooling and educational inequality: Socioeconomic disparities in children's learning. In J. Clark (Ed.), *James S. Coleman*. London: Falmer Press.

Ascher, C. (1988). Summer school, extended school year, and year-round schooling for disadvantaged students. *ERIC Clearinghouse on Urban Education Digest, 42*, 1–2.

Austin, G. R., Roger, B. G., & Walbesser, H. H. (1972). The effectiveness of summer compensatory education: A review of the research. *Review of Educational Research, 42*, 171–181.

Bowles, S., & Gintis, H. (1976). *Schooling in capitalist America*. New York: Basic Books.

Chmelynski, C. (1998). Summer school for meeting higher standards. *Education Digest, 63*, 47–50.

Cooper, H., Nye, B., Charlton, K., Lindsay, J., & Greathouse, S. (1996). The effects of summer vacation on achievement test scores: A narrative and meta-analytic review. *Review of Educational Research, 66*, 227–268.

Glass, G. V. (1976). Primary, secondary, and meta-analysis of research. *Educational Researcher, 5*, 3–8.

Heyns, B. (1978). *Summer learning and the effects of schooling.* New York: Academic Press.

Heyns, B. (1986). *Summer programs and compensatory education: The future of an idea.* New York. (ERIC Document Reproduction Service No. ED 293 906).

Jencks, C., & Phillips, M. (1998). *The Black-White test score gap.* Washington, DC: Brookings Institution Press.

Phillips, M., Crouse, J., & Ralph, J. (1998). Does the Black-White test score gap widen after children enter school? In C. Jencks & M. Phillips (Eds.), *The Black-White test score gap.* Washington, DC: Brookings Institution Press.

Raudenbush, S. W. (1994). Random effects models. In H. Cooper & L. V. Hedges (Eds.), *The handbook of research synthesis.* New York: Russell Sage Foundation.

Slavin, R. E. (1986). Best-evidence synthesis: An alternative to meta-analytic and traditional reviews. *Educational Researcher, 15*(9), 5–11.

**Harris Cooper** (Ph.D. 1975, University of Connecticut) is Professor of Psychology at the University of Missouri–Columbia. Dr. Cooper's research interests follow two paths. His book *Synthesizing Research: A Guide for Literature Reviews* is intended to teach advanced undergraduate and graduate students how to conduct all phases of research synthesis. He is also the editor, with Larry Hedges, of the *Handbook of Research Synthesis*. Dr. Cooper is also interested in the application of social psychology to educational policy issues. His research synthesis on homework was published as both a research monograph and a policy guide for school administrators, and he has also published in the area of teacher expectation effects. In 1984, Dr. Cooper received the first Raymond B. Cattell Early Career Award for Programmatic Research from the American Educational Research Association (AERA). He also won the AERA Award for Interpretive Scholarship in 1997.

**Kelly Charlton** (Ph.D. 1998, University of Missouri) is a Visiting Assistant Professor in the Psychology Department at the University of Missouri. Her research interests include the social psychology of education, and intra- and intergroup relationships.

**Jeffrey C. Valentine** (M.A. 1996, Northern Arizona University) is a graduate student in the Program in Social Psychology at the University of Missouri. His research interests include the social psychology of education, primary prevention programs for adolescents, and aggression.

**Laura Muhlenbruck** (M.A. 1999, University of Missouri) received a master's degree from the Program in Social Psychology at the University of Missouri. She is currently working toward her teaching certification in secondary English.

**Geoffrey D. Borman** (Ph.D. 1997, University of Chicago) is Associate Research Scientist at the Johns Hopkins University Center for Research on the Education of Students Placed at Risk (CRESPAR). He is particularly interested in applying quantitative methods to the study of programs and policies for students placed at risk, and in developing theoretical and empirical models for improving the educational opportunities and outcomes for poor and minority children. He is the editor, with Drs. Sam Stringfield and Robert Slavin, of a forthcoming book, *Title I: Compensatory Education at the Crossroads*, which documents the contributions, limitations, and future of the nation's largest compensatory education program.

# STATEMENT OF EDITORIAL POLICY

The *Monographs* series is intended as an outlet for major reports of developmental research that generate authoritative new findings and use these to foster a fresh and/or better integrated perspective on some conceptually significant issue or controversy. Submissions from programmatic research projects are particularly welcome; these may consist of individually or group-authored reports of findings from some single large-scale investigation or of a sequence of experiments centering on some particular question. Multiauthored sets of independent studies that center on the same underlying question can also be appropriate; a critical requirement in such instances is that the various authors address common issues and that the contribution arising from the set as a whole be both unique and substantial. In essence, irrespective of how it may be framed, any work that contributes significant data and/or extends developmental thinking will be taken under editorial consideration.

Submissions should contain a minimum of 80 manuscript pages (including tables and references); the upper limit of 150–175 pages is much more flexible (please submit four copies; a copy of every submission and associated correspondence is deposited eventually in the archives of the SRCD). Neither membership in the Society for Research in Child Development nor affiliation with the academic discipline of psychology is relevant; the significance of the work in extending developmental theory and in contributing new empirical information is by far the most crucial consideration. Because the aim of the series is not only to advance knowledge on specialized topics but also to enhance cross-fertilization among disciplines or subfields, it is important that the links between the specific issues under study and larger questions relating to developmental processes emerge as clearly to the general reader as to specialists on the given topic.

Potential authors who may be unsure whether the manuscript they are planning would make an appropriate submission are invited to draft an outline of what they propose and send it to the Editor for assessment. This mechanism, as well as a more detailed description of all editorial policies, evaluation processes, and format requirements, is given in the "Guidelines for the Preparation of *Monographs* Submissions," which can be obtained by contacting the Editor Designate, Willis Overton, Department of Psychology, 567 Weiss Hall, Temple University, Philadelphia, PA 19122 (e-mail: overton@vm.temple.edu).